D0910174

THAT THEY ALL MAY BE ONE

THAT THEY ALL MAY BE ONE

THE ENCOMPASSING COMMANDMENT TO BE ONE

LINDON J. ROBISON

That They All May Be One
Copyright © 2008 by Lindon J. Robison
All rights reserved

No part of this book may be reproduced in any form whatsoever, whether by graphic, visual, electronic, filming, microfilming, tape recording, or any other means, without the written permission of the author, except in the case of brief passages embodied in critical reviews and articles where the title, author, and ISBN accompany such a review or article.

Published and Distributed by:

Granite Publishing and Distribution, LLC
868 North 1430 West
Orem, Utah 84057
(801) 229-9023 • Toll Free (800) 574-5779
Fax (801) 229-1924

Cover Design: Steve Gray
Page Layout and Design: Lyndell Lutes

ISBN: 978-1-59936-024-9
Library of Congress Control Number: 2008927136
First Printing June 2008
10 9 8 7 6 5 4 3 2 1
Printed in the United States of America

TABLE OF CONTENTS

CR ဢ

PREFACE

ભ્ઉ

I asked one of my daughters for advice on how to write this book. ***"Make it real, make it relevant, and make it apply to me,"*** she demanded. So I asked myself, "How can I make this book about 'at-one-ment' real, relevant, and applicable to me, my family, and others?"

In an effort to comply with my daughter's request, I have drawn material from the experiences and efforts of our family, friends, and others, to become one. Then I told their stories through the lives of a fictitious family comprised of John and Amy and their children. Their successes and struggles to become one, I believe, will have a familiar ring because they are based on the experiences of real people—people like you and me. And if you can identify with John and Amy and with their family, then what they learn about "at-one-ment" will be real, relevant, and applicable to you as well. That is my hope—to help my loved ones and others avoid separations and sorrow and gain at-one-ments and joy.

ACKNOWLEDGMENTS

ℭℜℬ

First, I thank my sweetheart Bonnie for living the ways of at-one-ment and for being my inspiration for this book. Next, I thank our family and friends for providing me experiences and examples of at-one-ment to learn from and to write about. I also thank them for their suggestions on how to organize, edit, and better tell their stories. I thank Ken and Lyndell Lutes for their careful efforts to improve this work and prepare it for publication. Others who provided insights, needed corrections, and suggestions that improved the organization of this book include my sister Helen R. Findlay and my friends Brian Phillips, Wendy Moore, Jean Blake, David L. Draught, and David E. Spencer.

Finally, I excuse all my family members and friends for any errors that remain in this effort—for which I am solely responsible.

Prologue

TO BE ONE

ᦙ ᦧ

The Lord commands us to be one because, unless we are one with each other, we cannot be one with Him (see D&C 38:27). To this end the Savior prayed "that [we] all may be one" as He and His Father are one (John 17:21).

The state or condition of being one, at-one-ment, is the desired outcome of our Father in Heaven's plan of salvation. What makes our "at-one-ment" with God and each other possible is Christ's Atonement. According to Elder Bruce C. and Marie K. Hafen, "Jesus Christ came to accomplish the great at-one-ment, not the great alone-ment. He came to overcome our separation from God and from one another. He seeks to bring us to His Father, to Himself, and to each other, at one, through the gift and power of His Atonement. Even though we do need some space for ourselves, something deep inside each of us instinctively responds to this gospel of belonging, drawing us to certain other people and to God."[1]

Life is full of sorrows and separations, some avoidable and some not. Life can also be full of "at-one-ments" and joy. To enjoy at-one-ments we need to understand what it means to be one, with whom we are to be one, our needs for at-one-ment, and the blessings we receive when we are one. We also need to know how we sense at-one-ment, how we practice it, and how Christ's Atonement makes our at-one-ment possible. Answering these questions and reviewing prophetic prescriptions for at-one-ment is the focus of all that follows.

NOTES

1. Bruce C. and Marie K. Hafen, *The Belonging Heart: The Atonement and Relationships with God and Family,* (1994), 3.

Chapter One

THE COMMANDMENT—BE ONE

*Behold, this I have given unto you as a parable, and it
is even as I am. I say unto you, be one; and if
ye are not one ye are not mine*

—D&C 38:27

ᘓ ᘔ

To their ward members and friends, John and Amy appear to enjoy the ideal Latter-day Saint marriage. They have the outward signs of success. They drive nice cars, they live in a comfortable home in a safe neighborhood, and they enjoy friendly relations with their neighbors. Their children are happy and smart and—well—normal. And they hold responsible positions in their ward. Amy is the ward music and choir director and is widely admired for her talents. John is the ward Young Men's president and is popular among the youth. Yet, despite their outward signs of success, something isn't quite right in their marriage. Or, at least it is not as good as it could or should be.

Years of being distracted by the world, seeing imperfections in each other that weren't obvious when they married, and disagreeing over such things as budgets and how to raise their children sometimes separate them from each other and the excitement they enjoyed early in their marriage. And, sometimes they find themselves longing for those carefree days before they married and became responsible for bills, babies, and making each other happy.

John and Amy are both stressed. John worries about his job. Recently his supervisor criticized the production of his unit and made a veiled threat about his future with the company if things did not improve. Amy worries about confrontation. Before her marriage she tried to avoid confrontation. Now, it seems that her entire day is spent in confrontations—with one of her own children or one of the neighbor's children who loves to play in her yard. As a result, they both expect relief and comfort from each other at the end of the day and often fail to find it. They don't argue or disagree openly—they just don't connect as they had expected when they were married.

Lately, John and Amy have found Sunday School lessons something to be patiently endured. However, last Sunday's lesson caught their attention. The teacher, Brother Law, began the lesson by announcing, "Today we will study the encompassing commandment to 'be one.' The commandment is found several places, but most clearly in Doctrine and Covenants 38:27." He then looked at Amy and asked, "Amy, will you read for us?" Amy read, "Be one and if ye are not one ye are not mine." As she read she was convicted in her heart. At that moment she realized that she was not one—not with her best self, her husband, not with her friends and neighbors, and sometimes not even with God. This sinking feeling left her very unsettled, and she distracted herself to suppress the tears that she knew were coming.

John was also awakened from his musings by the scripture and reflected on his relationship with Amy. *Things between us have changed,* he thought to himself. *We don't talk anymore. We don't do things together. We don't have fun together. We're just not close like we once were.* Then he began to rationalize. *I'm sure we're just going through a stage in our marriage during which some separation is normal,* he thought to himself. *Don't all couples feel this way,* he asked himself? *Perhaps it is unrealistic to hope that the connections we felt early in our marriage would continue.*

For John and Amy, it was an uncomfortable moment when they both asked themselves in their hearts, *Are we one like the commandment requires?* And it hurt when they admitted to themselves, but not too each other, that indeed they lacked the "at-one-ment" required by the Lord. They both listened more intently to Brother Law's lesson.

Atonement and At-one-ment

Brother Law continued, "The success of our Father's plan of salvation and the commandment to be one requires that we achieve three at-one-ments...with our best selves (integrity), with others (Zion), and with God (eternal life). The truth is that these at-one-ments are realized together or not at all." Sister Quering raised her hand and without being called on asked, "What is the connection between the commandment to be one and Christ's Atonement?"

"To answer your question, Sister Quering," Brother Law responded, "we must understand two words that are naturally related, *atonement* and *at-one-ment*. The word *atonement* means literally to reconcile or to set 'at one' those who have been estranged.[1] The Atonement of Jesus Christ generally refers to 'that suffering endured, that power displayed, and that love manifested by the Savior in three principal locations, namely, the Garden of Gethsemane, the cross of Calvary, and the tomb of Arimathaea.'[2] *At-one-ment,* on the other hand, refers to the state or condition of being one, united, or reconciled with others.[3] Christ's Atonement makes our at-one-ment with our Christlike selves, each other, and God possible after all that we can do" (2 Nephi 25:23).

Then Brother Law approached the chalk board. "We cannot possibly keep the commandment to be one unless we more fully comprehend the depth and the breadth of the commandment. Consider what the Savior and His prophets have taught about the commandment to be one." Brother Law paused to allow class members to turn to John 17:20–22. Then he explained the meaning of the verses.

"In the Savior's intercessory prayer prior to His atoning sacrifice, in the Garden of Gethsemane He prayed for the at-one-ment of His disciples and those who would believe on their words… 'Neither pray I for these alone, but for them also which shall believe on me through their word; that they all may be one; as thou, Father, art in me, and I in thee, that they also may be one in us: that the world may believe that thou hast sent me. And the glory which thou gavest me I have given them; that they may be one, even as we are one' (John 17:20–22).

"Christ's prayer for the at-one-ment of His disciples on that night of infinite sorrow and suffering may have been all the more poignant and pleading because one of His own, Judas Iscariot, had already betrayed Him, and the chief among His own disciples was about to desert Him. No wonder His prayer was focused on the at-one-ment of his disciples.

"In the New World following His Atonement and Resurrection, the Savior explained that the intent of His Nephite mission was to bring His followers to at-one-ment as a good shepherd gathers his sheep…'But I have received a commandment of the Father that I shall go unto them, and that they shall hear my voice, and shall be numbered among my sheep, that there may be one fold and one shepherd' (3 Nephi 16:3).

"The Savior taught that the process of bringing His people to at-one-ment would continue in the resurrection. 'For a trump shall sound both long and loud, even as upon Mount Sinai, and all the earth shall quake, and they shall come forth—yea, even the dead which died in me, to receive a crown of righteousness, and to be clothed upon, even as I am, to be with me, that we may be one' (D&C 29:13).

"At-one-ment is the defining characteristic of Christ's disciples. 'If we are not one, we are not His!' Indeed, it is the commandment that includes all others. As a result, not only did Christ preach at-one-ment, but so did His holy Apostles. Paul taught this need for at-one-ment to the Romans. 'Now the God of patience and consolation grant you to be likeminded one toward another according to Christ Jesus: that ye may with one mind and one mouth glorify God, even the Father of our Lord Jesus Christ. Wherefore receive ye one another, as Christ also received us to the glory of God' (Romans 15:5–7).

"Before he died, Lehi pleaded with his family to be one. 'And now that my soul might have joy in you, and that my heart might leave this world with gladness because of you, that I might not be brought down with grief and sorrow to the grave, arise from the dust, my sons, and be men, and be determined in one mind and in one heart, united in all things, that ye may not come down into captivity' (2 Nephi 1:21)."

At this point in Brother Law's lesson, John and Amy wondered why the doctrine of at-one-ment seemed so new. Had it been taught before and they weren't paying attention? Or had they ignored the doctrine because until now, it didn't seem so important?

Brother Law continued, "Alma taught at the waters of Mormon that at-one-ment was a requirement for baptism (see Mosiah 18:8–10). He emphasized that among those entering into the waters of baptism, there should be no contention 'but that they should look forward with one eye, having one faith and one baptism, having their hearts knit together in unity and in love one towards another' (Mosiah 18:21).

"In a revelation to Joseph Smith, the Savior promised...'I am Jesus Christ, the Son of God, who was crucified for the sins of the world, even as many as will believe on my name, that they may become the sons of God, even one in me as I am one in the Father, as the Father is one in me, that we may be one' (D&C 35:2).

"Brigham Young also emphasized at-one-ment. 'How pleasing it is for brethren to dwell together in unity. Let the Saints of the most high ever cultivate this principle, and the most glorious blessings must result not only to them individually, but to the whole church' (HC 4:226–232).

"President Ezra Taft Benson taught…'If there be any division among us, let us set aside anything of this kind and join ranks in the great responsibility to move forward the work of the Lord. If there be those who have become disaffected, we reach out to you…and stand ready to assist and welcome you back in full fellowship and activity in the Church.'[4] Finally, President Gordon B. Hinckley reflected on the blessing that could belong to the saints when they are truly united…'When people of goodwill labor cooperatively in an honest and dedicated way, there is no end to what they can accomplish.'"[5]

The bell rang, signaling the end of Sunday School, and Brother Law concluded his lesson by expressing his conviction that the essence of gospel living was keeping the encompassing commandment to "be one." After class, John and Amy sat pensively wondering, *Where do we go from here?* They both wondered if the other felt the same way. They both had so many questions and concerns. And through a "glass darkly" they could also see wonderful opportunities for increased joy if they could regain the at-one-ment they felt was missing in their marriage.

Why Study At-one-ment?

We study at-one-ment because we are all like John and Amy and suffer because of our separations. Our separations and "alonements" may be different than the ones they suffer, but their pains of separation feel much the same for each of us. Therefore, we study at-one-ment to learn how to avoid separations when possible and how to be made better by them when they cannot be avoided.

We study at-one-ment because all that is meaningful requires that each one of us be one with our best selves—a person of integrity. John and Amy may have been surprised to know that at-one-ment with others begins with our being one with our best selves. Only after we have become persons of integrity can we become one with others and God. Shakespeare described this internal at-one-ment that leads to at-one-ment with others—"To thine own self be true and it follows as the night the day, thou canst not be false to any man."[6]

Finally, we study at-one-ment because an all wise and loving Heavenly Father commands us to be one. Our faith in and our love for Him is therefore reflected in our at-one-ment, our keeping of His commandment to be one.

A Personal Note

The first time I recall being aware of the pain of separation occurred over fifty years ago. I can still remember sitting in the old Fillmore First Ward building. I was alone and crying during the funeral of my kind Aunt Fern. One reason I felt so alone was because Aunt Fern was like the hub of a wheel. Her efforts kept so many of us connected. I remember so often seeing her black and white Buick parked in front of the houses of Aunt Neva, Uncle Gene, or my own, and in front of the house of any one really in need.

My mother dearly loved her older sister Fern, and part of my pain was for my mother. But I grieved for myself as well, because I knew that things very important to me would be different without Aunt Fern. Since then, I have reflected on the painful feelings caused by separations again and again as each new separation from a loved one has filled me with the same feelings of sadness that I experienced at Aunt Fern's funeral.

The opposite of separations and sadness are at-one-ments, re-unions, and joy. I remember a few short years ago, with all of our family together at the Detroit International Airport, we welcomed our youngest son Nathan home from the Russia Samara Mission. What pure joy we experienced as our rugged-handsome son emerged through the gate. We hugged, my wife Bonnie cried, and the grandchildren held up signs saying, Welcome home Nathan! These and other wonderful reunions have filled me with wonder at the joy that comes when we keep the commandment to be one.

Conclusions

The breadth of the commandment to be one is such that it covers all of the others. Indeed, it may be that all commandments are simply detailed instructions on how to be one. At-one-ment is at the core of our gospel living and the reason for Christ's atoning sacrifice. Furthermore, success in our mortal state depends on our achieving at-one-ment, without which our divided kingdoms and homes cannot stand (see Mark 3:24–27). Therefore, the study and application of the principles of at-one-ment merit our most careful concentration, partly because there is so much joy to be experienced once we learn about and keep the commandment to be one.

NOTES

1. Bible Dictionary, 617.

2. Tad Callister, *Infinite Atonement*, (2000), 23.

3. Hugh Nibley, *Approaching Zion*, (1989), 556.

4. Sheri L. Dew, *Ezra Taft Benson: A Biography*, (1987), 494.

5. Gordon B. Hinckley, "Some Lessons I Learned as a Boy," *Ensign,* May 1993, 54.

6. William Shakespeare, *Hamlet, act 1, scene 3.*

Chapter Two

AT-ONE-MENT AND JOY

Joy is the ultimate sensation of well-being.
It comes from being complete and in harmony
with our Creator and his eternal laws
—Dallin H. Oaks

☙ ❧

Amy and Jane were the best of friends. Their at-one-ment was a continual source of joy—their disagreement and separations, a source of sadness. Days after Brother Law's Sunday School lesson on the commandment to "be one," Amy reminisced about her friendship with Jane. Then she wrote the following entry in her journal:

> *Growing up, Jane was my only LDS friend with whom I felt really close. We had similar interests, values, and sense of fashion. Even though we went to two different high schools, lived in separate towns, and were not the same age (she was 2 years older), we were best friends. One evening during our high school years, we decided to go to a church dance. Jane had her driver's license and a car, so she came and picked me up.*
>
> *On the way to the church dance I asked if we could stop by a school friend's house. She was having a party and I felt obligated to stop in for a minute and say "Hi." Jane asked me if I wanted her to come in or if I wanted to just go alone. I thought about it and decided I really wanted to go to the dance and knew that if we both went in it would take much longer than if I just*

popped in really fast. That was the plan I told her. She sat in the car and waited. I ran in and said "Hi" to a few people and was back—not as quickly as I wanted, but pretty quick all the same.

Then we left for the church. But Jane had become distant. I tried to understand why, but I had no idea. I knew it had something to do with stopping at my friend's house and assumed she felt like I had just taken too long. I apologized profusely, but to no avail. When we arrived at the stake center, Jane let me out and drove away with no explanation. For the next several days and weeks, Jane didn't return my phone calls. At seminary, she made fun of me and refused to talk to my face.

I was heart-broken. I didn't know what I had done and I couldn't seem to be able to fix it. But I was also defensive. I figured I hadn't really done anything that wrong—a little late maybe, but nothing that deserved this kind of treatment. I was lonely, sad, and angry. I was also miserable. I remember those few weeks of my life as a dark, dark time. Even though no one else knew what had happened, at school I felt as if I had no friends—that I was basically a "loser." It seemed that our separation had affected my whole life.

Then one Sunday we had a fireside at her house. Jane and I spent the entire time upstairs in her room, as I recall, screaming at each other. She finally explained her side of things. She had been offended because she thought I considered her not cool enough to go to my friend's party. Finally, I was also able to explain my side of things—that nothing was further from the truth. I thought she was way more fun than my friends at the party and that what I had really wanted was to spend the evening doing the things we love to do instead of hanging out with school friends. When we finally worked out our differences, there was a new depth to our relationship. We trusted each other more. Some of our teenage insecurity was gone. She explained she had talked with her mom and that her mom asked her if the offense was worth losing a friend. For a while, she thought about it and in the end decided our relationship was more important than her feelings. She apologized. And I did too.

Our friendship has been a great source of joy for both of us. When her two brothers died in a terrible car accident, I was able to be there to provide some measure of comfort. Through my long years of being single, she was a true friend involving me in her life with her husband and kids. We have lived hundreds of miles away from each other, have had lots of disagreements and arguments, but ever since the high school blow-out, we have remained close friends.

Amy closed her journal and reflected for a moment. Then a sudden thought came to her, more as a feeling than a thought, *At-one-ment leads to joy; and that's why God commands us to be one.* Armed with this new insight, Amy began to consider the insights others had gained on the connection between joy and at-one-ment.

Harmony with God and Joy

Harmony is a synonym for at-one-ment. In music, harmony refers to notes in a musical selection that together in at-one-ment produce a pleasing sound. In literature, harmony refers to an interweaving, an at-one-ment, of different accounts into a single consistent narrative. And between people, harmony refers to agreement, mutual caring, shared vision, or synergistic efforts that produce peace.

Elder Dallin H. Oaks explained that "joy is the ultimate sensation of well-being. It comes from being complete and in *harmony* with our Creator and his eternal laws. The opposite of joy is misery. Misery is more than unhappiness, sorrow, or suffering. Misery is the ultimate state of disharmony with God and his laws" (emphasis added).[2]

C.S. Lewis described how joy requires us to be in harmony with God. "[Some] seek to invent some sort of happiness for themselves without God. And out of that hopeless attempt has come nearly all that we call human history—money, poverty, ambition, war, prostitution, classes, slavery—the long terrible story of people trying to find something other than God which will make them happy. The reason why it can never succeed is this. God made us—invented us as a man invents an engine. A car is made to run on gasoline, and it would not run properly on anything else. Now God designed the human machine to run on Himself. He Himself is the fuel our spirits were designed to burn, or the food our spirits were designed to feed on. There is no other. That is why it is just no good asking God to make us happy in our own way without bothering about religion. God cannot give us a happiness and peace apart from Himself, because it is not there. There is no such thing."[3]

Harmony with God is to our joy as water is to the survival of fish. Outside of the water, a miserable fish flops around seeking survival in a foreign environment for which it was not designed. Outside of harmony with God, we fuss and fret, looking for joy in an environment for which we were not designed to exist.

Harmony with God's Plan of Happiness and Joy

To direct our efforts toward at-one-ment and joy, our Father in Heaven provided us a plan. He called His plan, the plan of happiness because our joy was its desired outcome (see Alma 42:8, 16). To realize a fulness of joy, His plan provided for our immortality and eternal life, our at-one-ment with Him (see Moses 1:39). When we heard our Father's plan for us to become like Him and live with Him, "we shouted for joy" (Job 38:7).

Progress and Joy

An essential insight found in the plan of happiness is that progress toward at-one-ment with God and joy travel together or not at all. The poet William Butler Yeats captured this truth when he penned the lines, "Happiness is neither virtue nor pleasure nor this thing nor that, but simply growth. We are happy when we are growing."[4] Thus, another name for God's plan of happiness is the plan of eternal progression.

For reasons not yet revealed, our Father's plan required that Adam and Eve break a lesser commandment of God to keep a more important one. By partaking of the forbidden fruit they opened the door to their (and our) progress toward at-one-ment with God by providing them (and us) the moral agency to choose between right and wrong, and to progress by choosing the right. Choosing the right led them progressively back to be with and like God.

Had Adam and Eve not transgressed and remained in a state of innocence without the opportunity to progress, we could not have progressed either nor could we have experienced true joy. Lehi explained, "And they would have had no children; wherefore they would have remained in a state of innocence, having no joy, for they knew no misery; doing no good, for they knew no sin" (2 Nephi 2:23). Adam confirmed that joy and progress travel together or not at all. "Blessed be the name of God, for because of my transgression my eyes are opened, and in this life I shall have joy, and again in the flesh I shall see God" (Moses 5:10).

God's Commandments and Joy

God included in the plan of happiness ordinances and commandments designed to lead man to at-one-ment with Him (eternal life) and joy. Joseph Smith explained that "happiness is the object and design of our existence; and will be the end thereof, if we pursue the path that leads to it... and that God will never institute an ordinance or give a commandment to his people that are not calculated in its nature to promote their happiness."[5]

Along our path toward at-one-ment with God, we make mistakes and sometimes sin. When we do, God commands us to repent, change, restore, recognize our error, and appeal to God's grace to repay and repair the wrongs we cannot undo ourselves. This progressive act is at first painful, but in the end is a great source of joy.

Alma the Younger described the joy that followed his repentance and the forgiveness that brought him to at-one-ment with God. "I cried within my heart: O Jesus, thou Son of God, have mercy on me, who am in the gall of bitterness, and am encircled about by the everlasting chains of death. And now, behold, when I thought this, I could remember my pains no more; yea, I was harrowed up by the memory of my sins no more. And oh, what joy, and what marvelous light I did behold; yea, my soul was filled with joy as exceeding as was my pain! Yea, I say unto you, my son, that there could be nothing so exquisite and so bitter as were my pains. Yea, and again I say unto you, my son, that on the other hand, there can be nothing so exquisite and sweet as was my joy" (Alma 36:18–21).

Meeting the Tests of Life and Joy

In God's plan of happiness, we progress toward at-one-ment with Him when we face life's tests successfully by choosing to do right rather than wrong, even when it is difficult to do so. Barbara Winder, former general president of the Relief Society, described how Joseph Smith met life's tests successfully under difficult circumstances and found joy.

> Near the end of his life, having experienced years of trial, almost beyond our ability to comprehend, being dragged through the streets, tarred and feathered, having some of his closest associates turn against him, the Prophet Joseph Smith could yet testify and cheer us on as he exclaimed: 'Now, what do we hear in the gospel which we have received? A voice of gladness! A voice of mercy from heaven; ... a voice of gladness for the living and the dead; glad tidings of great joy.... Let your hearts rejoice, and be exceedingly glad' (D&C 128:19, 22).[6]

We may sometimes ask, "Why must our tests be so difficult?" An analogy may provide the answer. Suppose I find an attractive tie in the clothing store and approach the clerk, intent on making the tie my own. Then, I look at the price tag. It is expensive. Now I find out how much I value the tie. Only if the tie is worth more to me than the money I must sacrifice to buy it do I make the purchase.

Likewise, we may never know how much we value eternal life and joy until we are asked to make significant sacrifices to acquire it. Elder Reed Smoot explained, "Be not dismayed at the trials of life; they are sent for our good. God knows what keys in the human soul to touch in order to draw out its sweetest and most perfect harmonies. These may be the strains of sadness and sorrow as well as the loftier notes of joy and gladness." [7]

Bringing Others to Christ and Joy

God designed His plan of happiness to bring to pass the exaltation and eternal life of man. To be in harmony with God requires that we have this same purpose, to assist in bringing men and women to eternal life and exaltation. The Lord described to Joseph Smith the joy that we can experience as we bring others to Christ. "And if it so be that you should labor all your days in crying repentance unto this people, and bring, save it be one soul unto me, how great shall be your joy with him in the kingdom of my Father! And now, if your joy will be great with one soul that you have brought unto me into the kingdom of my Father, how great will be your joy if you should bring many souls unto me!" (D&C 18:15–16).

Helaman described the joy his people felt as they brought souls to Christ. "The people of the church did have great joy because of the conversion of the Lamanites, yea, because of the church of God, which had been established among them. And they did fellowship one with another, and did rejoice one with another, and did have great joy" (Helaman 6:3).

Marriage and Joy

The purpose of our Father in Heaven's plan of happiness is for us to become one with Him and to be like Him. He is our Heavenly Father and "truth eternal tells me I've a mother there."[8] Thus, to become like God requires that we become one with our spouse. Indeed, the at-one-ment found in a righteous marriage is an essential part of God's plan of happiness.

The Lord explained, "Marriage is ordained of God unto man...that the earth might answer the end of its creation; and that it might be filled with the measure of man, according to his creation before the world was made" (D&C 49:15–17). The Apostle Paul taught "neither is the man without the woman, neither the woman without the man, in the Lord" (1 Corinthians 11:11). President Spencer W. Kimball said, "Without proper and successful marriage, one will never be exalted." [9]

Joy and the Witness of the Holy Ghost

To help us achieve the at-one-ment and joy intended by the plan of happiness, God gave us the gift of the Holy Ghost. As we travel through life attempting to reach at-one-ment, the Holy Ghost comforts, guides, teaches, and witnesses of the truth that joy is found in God's plan of happiness.

Through the Holy Ghost, we may know "the truth of all things" (Moroni 10:5). Through its power, we receive a testimony of Jesus Christ. "No man can say that Jesus is the Lord, but by the Holy Ghost" (1 Corinthians 12:3). More importantly, it is the companionship of the Holy Ghost that fills our hearts with joy and peace. The Apostle Paul taught, "Now the God of hope fill you with all joy and peace in believing, that ye may abound in hope, through the power of the Holy Ghost" (Romans 15:13). "For the kingdom of God is not meat and drink; but righteousness, and peace, and joy in the Holy Ghost" (Romans 14:17). Elder Parley

P. Pratt characterized the gift of the Holy Ghost as "joy to the heart, [and] light to the eyes."[10]

Love and Joy

The most descriptive attribute that can be applied to God and therefore the most essential for us to acquire if we are to become like Him is love, for God is love (see 1 John 4:7–8). Therefore, to be like God and gain eternal life we must be filled with love. And when we are filled with love, we have joy.

Elder Jeffrey and Sister Patricia Holland explained, "Joy comes from loving and being loved. When this divine attribute is at work in our feelings for our family, our neighbors, our God, *and ourselves,* we feel joy. When it is immobilized with conflict toward others, toward God, or toward ourselves, we are depressed in our growth and we become depressed in our attitude."[11]

The love of God that fills us with joy was described in a vision as the fruit of the tree of life. Nephi related, "And the angel said unto me: Behold the Lamb of God, yea, even the Son of the Eternal Father! Knowest thou the meaning of the tree which thy father saw? And I answered him, saying: Yea, it is the love of God, which sheddeth itself abroad in the hearts of the children of men; wherefore, it is the most desirable above all things. And he spake unto me, saying: Yea, and the most joyous to the soul" (1 Nephi 11:21–23).

Being Gathered and Joy

Our joy is increased when we are gathered together with those we love. We sing:

Oh, what songs of the heart
We shall sing all the day,
When again we assemble at home,
When we meet ne'er to part
With the blest o'er the way,
There no more from our loved ones to roam!

When we meet ne'er to part,
Oh, what songs of the heart
We shall sing in our beautiful home.[12]

On the other hand, when we are separated from those we love
and serve, we experience intense sorrow. A recent event recounted
by Elder Dallin H. Oaks illustrates both the sorrow of separations
and the joy of reunions.

> As part of an outing, a group of Latter-day Saint Boy Scouts
> entered an abandoned mine in the mountains not far from here.
> Somehow, young Joshua Dennis was separated from the group
> and became lost in the mine. Anyone who has ever lost some-
> thing valuable will remember that terrible feeling. The pain is
> most extreme when we have lost a loved one. Joshua's family
> and friends feared their loss might be permanent.
>
> Search efforts were organized. For days, many good people
> dropped everything they were doing to search for the one who
> was lost. Many shared the pain of his loss. Then, miraculously,
> he was found. Prayers were answered, and the mercy of a loving
> Heavenly Father was manifest in the happiness of family and
> friends reunited with the one who was lost. The pain of loss
> turned to the overwhelming joy of reunion.[13]

The scriptures provide other examples of joy found in reunions
of loved ones. When Nephi and his brothers returned from Jerusalem with brass plates, the scriptures record, "And it came to pass that
after we had come down into the wilderness unto our father, behold,
he was filled with joy, and also my mother, Sariah, was exceedingly
glad, for she truly had mourned because of us" (1 Nephi 5:1).

At-one-ment with the Mind of the Lord and Joy

One way we will come to at-one-ment with God and His plan
of happiness is to understand His answers to important questions.
Coming to an increased understanding of God's mind also fills us
with joy (see D&C 42:68–69).

Oliver Cowdery described the joy he felt as he became acquainted with the mind of the Lord as revealed truths fell from the lips of the Prophet Joseph Smith. "These were days never to be forgotten—to sit under the sound of a voice dictated by the inspiration of heaven, awakened the utmost gratitude of this bosom!"[14]

Jeremiah wrote of his joy found in being at-one with the mind of the Lord. "Thy word was unto me the joy and rejoicing of mine heart" (Jeremiah 15:16). Because the scriptures bring us to harmony with God in our minds, they are often referred to as "glad tidings of great joy" (Helaman 16:14; Mosiah 3:3; Alma 13:22; see also Luke 2:10). As we learn and abide their teachings, that joy becomes part of our lives. John expressed the joy that comes when our children are guided by the truth of God's goodness. "I have no greater joy than to hear that my children walk in truth" (3 John 1:4).

Sorrowful Separations

The Sorrow of Alone-ment

Joy and at-one-ments with God, man, and our best self are eternal companions. So are separations and sorrow. One reason that joy and at-one-ment are so important is because their alternative—sorrow and separation—are so awful. The sorrowful state of those lacking at-one-ment was described by the philosopher Eric Fromm.

"Man is gifted with reason; he is life being aware of itself; he has awareness of himself, of his fellowmen, of his past, and of the possibilities of his future. This awareness of himself as a separate entity, the awareness of his own short life span, . . . of his helplessness before the forces of nature and of society, all this makes his separate disunited existence an unbearable prison. He would become insane could he not liberate himself from this prison and reach out, unite himself in some form or other with men, the world outside."[15]

Referring to the consequences of separations, especially during war, Hobbes wrote that when "men live without other security than what their own strength and their own invention shall furnish them ... the life of man [is] solitary, poor, nasty, brutish, and short."[16]

Substitute Connections with the World

Those who lack at-one-ment with others, their best self, and God often search for joy in worldly substitutes. These substitute sources of joy may include such things as one's work, positions held, honors won, degrees earned, wealth accumulated, or power exercised—things that become more important than people.

Jesus warned His disciples not to look for meaning in one's temporary connection to the world. "And he said unto them, Take heed, and beware of covetousness: for a man's life consisteth not in the abundance of the things which he possesseth" (Luke 12:15).

Separated from the presence of God, the world to which Adam and Eve were banished was described as lone and dreary. This nickname for the world—lone and dreary—forever connected these most miserable of companions. If we want to know what causes sorrow and how to avoid it, we need look no further than separations.

Sin and Separations

Some sorrowful separations are temporary in nature and result from the conditions of the world in which we live. These, however, are mostly physical separations and thankfully are often followed with a reunion. However, the most significant sorrow-filled separations are produced by sin—knowing God's commandments and rebelling against them (see James 4:17). Isaiah described the spiritual separation between man and God that occurs as a result of sin. "Your iniquities have separated between you and your God, and your sins have hid his face from you, that he will not hear" (Isaiah 59:2).

To emphasize the seriousness of man's separation from the influence and sustaining power of God, this sin caused separation is called a spiritual death. Alma taught, "And now behold, I say unto you then cometh a death, even a second death, which is a spiritual death; then is a time that whosoever dieth in his sins, as to a temporal death, shall also die a spiritual death; yea, he shall die as to things pertaining unto righteousness" (Alma 12:16). The sorrow associated with spiritual death was described by Lehi. "And men are instructed sufficiently that they know good from evil. And the law is given unto men. And by the law no flesh is justified; or, by the law men are cut off. Yea, by the temporal law they were cut off; and also, by the spiritual law they perish from that which is good, and become miserable forever" (2 Nephi 2:5).

Sin is a hostile act that places us in opposition to God and is motivated by the self-deception that there is another way besides God's way to joy. In the premortal world, Satan knew God's will and rebelled against it. Not only did he rebel against God, but he sought to lead others in rebellion against God. Satan stirred up others to rebellion against God to share in his misery because even the miserable love company (see 2 Nephi 2:27).

Reunions without Harmony

While harmonious reunions bring joy, reunions with those with whom we are "out-of-tune" bring discomfort and misery. Indeed, it was the thought of such a reunion that filled Alma's soul with eternal torment. Alma wrote of this reunion, "I was racked with eternal torment, for my soul was harrowed up to the greatest degree and racked with all my sins.... the very thought of coming into the presence of my God did rack my soul with inexpressible horror" (Alma 36: 12,14).

When separations and sorrow are such awful traveling companions, we may wonder why we so frequently invite them to join us on our journey through life. One answer is because of Satan's capacity to desensitize our spirits. And when desensitized, we become past feeling and cannot experience or long for the at-one-ment and love from which we once derived so much joy. But at last, all will discover the eternal truth that *"wickedness never was happiness"* (Alma 41:10; emphasis added).

☜ ☞

Amy picked up the phone—it was Jane. "Jane!" she exclaimed, "I was just thinking about you. It's so good to hear your voice." Jane answered, "See, that's what you get when you think about me, I call." Amy chuckled. Then they chatted for a few minutes about their children, their siblings, their husbands, what they were planning for dinner, and about nothing important. Then they said goodbye and Amy hung up the phone. But for a moment she basked in a happy kind of feeling that comes from knowing you have a true friend who really cares.

Conclusions

Harmony and at-one-ment are made possible because of Christ's birth, Atonement, Resurrection, and gospel. Thus, we celebrate His birth by singing, "Joy to the world, the Lord is come."

Sin separates us from God, others, and our best selves. Through Christ's Atonement and our repentance, we can re-establish our lost at-one-ment and find joy. King Benjamin taught, "And the Lord God hath sent his holy prophets among all the children of men, to declare these things to every kindred, nation, and tongue, that thereby whosoever should believe that Christ should come, the same might receive remission of their sins, and rejoice with exceedingly great joy, even as though he had already come among them" (Mosiah 3:13).

NOTES

1. Dallin H. Oaks, "Joy and Mercy," *Ensign*, November1991, 73.

2. Ibid.

3. C. S. Lewis, *Mere Christianity*, (1952), 53–54.

4. William Butler Yeats, www.famouspoetsandpoems.com/poets.

5. *Teachings of the Prophet Joseph Smith*, sel. Joseph Fielding Smith (1976), 256.

6. Barbara W. Winder, "Finding Joy in Life," *Ensign*, November 1987, 95.

7. Reed Smoot, "Joy," *Ensign*, October 1972, 16.

8. "O My Father," *Hymns of The Church of Jesus Christ of Latter-day Saints*, no. 292.

9. Spencer W. Kimball, *Marriage and Divorce*, (1976), 24; quoted by Dallin H. Oaks, "The Great Plan of Happiness," *Ensign*, November 1993, 72.

10. Parley P. Pratt, *Key to the Science of Theology: A Voice of Warning*, (reprinted 1978); quoted by James E. Faust, "The Light in Their Eyes," *Ensign*, November 2005, 20.

11. Jeffrey R. Holland and Patricia T. Holland, *On Earth As It Is in Heaven*, (1989), 68.

12. "Oh, What Songs of the Heart," *Hymns of The Church of Jesus Christ of Latter-day Saints*, no. 286.

13. Dallin H. Oaks, "Joy and Mercy," *Ensign*, November 1991, 73.

14. *Pearl of Great Price*; JS-History Note: 2: 1.

15. Eric Fromm, *The Art of Loving*, (1956), 17.

16. Thomas Hobbes, *Leviathan*, Part 1, Chapter XIII, 1651.

Chapter Three

OBJECTS OF AT-ONE-MENT

*In order to experience true joy...at least three
factors are needed. You need to feel good about
the people with whom you live and work—your
companions in life. You must feel good about yourself—not in any sense of conceit, but simply a
proper esteem for yourself, well deserved. And
possibly most important, you must feel good about
your relation to God and sincerely love Him.*

—Russell M. Nelson

Ꮳ ᏒᏛ

It was late Saturday afternoon when Amy answered Jill's
phone call. The voice at the other end was raspy and la-
bored. Even still, Amy could recognize that it was her friend Jill.
Speaking with obvious pain, Jill lamented, "Amy, I need your help.
I am supposed to teach the Beehives tomorrow and I can hardly
talk. If Fred brings over the manual, could you sub for me?" Amy
hated these last-minute assignments. But, she also knew that Jill
would never call her unless it was truly an emergency. She racked
her brain for an excuse, but sympathy for Jill and her long training
to not turn down assignments led her to say, "Of course, Jill, I will
be happy to help out."

Later that evening when all the children were in bed and John
was engrossed in one of the March Madness playoff games, Amy
finally had time to read from Jill's Beehive manual. As she began

reading, Amy found that the lesson focused on the World War II experiences of Wilson P. Lauitzen. His World War II experiences illustrated how at-one-ment with God leads to at-one-ment with others, even enemy soldiers. She read the following account:

> We were fighting in the 'Battle of the Bulge' near the town of Ammonius, Belgium. By that time the Germans were on the defensive. We had just succeeded in cutting off or surrounding a sector of the German line. They were surrendering in large numbers. As we were disarming the soldiers, one of them said to me in broken English: 'Would you know if there are any Mormon soldiers in your unit?' I replied, 'Yes, I am a Mormon.' He asked, 'Do you hold the priesthood?' 'Yes, I do,' I answered. 'I was married in the temple.' 'Would you be so kind as to come with me to that shell hole over there and administer to my buddy? He is pretty well shaken up, and pretty badly wounded.' Of course I consented to go. We found that his buddy was in a bad condition and was suffering much pain. Then the two of us, who a few short hours before had been on the opposite sides in the bitter struggle, knelt down and administered to the wounded lad. And as we did so, I felt the spirit of the Lord very strongly. I know that that feeling was shared by them, too. As we finished, the litter-bearers were there. We lifted the broken body to the stretcher. Then our ways parted: the wounded boy was taken to the hospital, the German soldier was sent back with the other prisoners, and I went on with my other duties.[2]

Amy continued reading her manual. The commandment to "be one" requires an object. With whom are we to be one? The scriptures are clear on who should be the objects of our at-one-ment. We are to be one with our best selves, each other, and God. In the case of Brother Lauitzen, he became one with an enemy soldier because of their common connection to the Savior and their integrity. Their common connection bonded them together as brothers even though they wore the uniforms of warring nations.

Of course, the three at-one-ments with self, others, and God are connected. We cannot be one with others without first becoming persons of integrity. On the other hand, we cannot be one with others and become a Zion people unless we follow the same shepherd, worship the same God, and acknowledge our shared spiritual heritage. In short, at-one-ment among our brothers and sisters requires at-one-ment with God.

Amy closed the manual. *Of course,* she thought to herself. *Be one with my best self, then with John and others, and then with God. Or perhaps, I must first work on becoming one with God?* She knew she had made an important discovery. *I am not really doing my part to be one with God,* she reflected. She recalled the times when her evening prayers were distracted and insincere— nights when she was so tired that she just wanted to get it over and get into bed. And scripture reading? When was there any time? *The baby is up before I have a chance to read,* she rationalized. But Amy knew in her heart that God would make it possible for her to keep the prophet's plea to read the scriptures daily if she would do her part. At that moment she resolved in her heart to do better.

At-one-ment with God and One's Best Self

We need to know whose we are before we can answer the question, with whom am I one? *Tarzan of the Apes* by Edgar Rice Burroughs tells of an orphan raised in the African jungles by a mother ape. This interesting story focuses on the difficulties Tarzan faced because he did not know who were his parents—apes or humans? Tarzan's discovery of his human heritage had a profound impact on him because it changed how he related to both animals and humans. The story emphasizes an important point—we are unlikely to ever know who we are and where we belong until we know to whom we belong.[3]

The need to know whose we are before we can know who we are, is captured by the scriptural quote from Jesus, "And this is life eternal, that they might know thee the only true God, and Jesus Christ, whom thou hast sent" (John 17:3). Elder Neal A. Maxwell taught, "Remember the popular lines in *Fiddler on the Roof* about Anatevka? There, 'everyone knows who he is and what God expects him to do,' to which might be added 'and what God expects him to be.'"[4]

The need to know whose we are before knowing who we are also explains why the first and great commandment is to love the Lord with all of our heart, mind, might, and strength—a commandment that requires knowledge of God and His attributes and His plan for us, His children. One answer to the question of whose we are is contained in the lyrics to a favorite hymn. "I am a child of God and he has sent me here . . . [and] if I, but learn to do his will I'll live with him once more."[5]

Finally, the need to know whose we are before we can answer the question, with whom am I to be one? explains why the Restoration of the gospel of Jesus Christ began with God the Father and His Son Jesus Christ revealing themselves and their character to the boy Joseph Smith. Armed with an understanding of whose he was, Joseph Smith was empowered to effect the Restoration of the gospel despite intense persecution. Understanding the need to know whose we are helps us appreciate why the first lesson that missionaries teach investigators emphasizes that God is our loving Heavenly Father (Acts 17:29). The need to know whose we are also helps us understand why the first Article of Faith describes our belief in the existence and separate identity of each member of the Godhead.

Knowledge of our divine parentage satisfies our deepest needs, to be loved and to be valued. We know God loves us because He "gave his only begotten Son, that whosoever believeth in him should not perish, but have everlasting life" (John 3:16). We know that we have great worth because "the worth of souls is great in the sight of God" (D&C 18:10). And because the worth of souls is great, the greatest work we can do "is to declare repentance unto this people, that [we] may bring souls unto [God], that [we] may rest with them in the kingdom of [our] Father" (D&C 16:6).

Knowledge of God the Father and Jesus Christ also teaches us what we can become—perfect like Them (see Matthew 5:48; 3 Nephi 12:48). With this knowledge we know who we can call on for help. "Look unto God with firmness of mind, and pray unto him with exceeding faith, and he will console you in your afflictions" (Jacob 3:1). Also with this knowledge we know whose example we should follow. "For the works which [Christ] did are the ones we should also do" (3 Nephi 27:21). With this knowledge we know to whom we owe our souls. We belong to God "for [w]e are bought with a price" (1 Corinthians 6:20).

Knowledge of the only true God and Jesus Christ teaches us of our true relationship to each other. We are brothers and sisters and equally loved by our Father in Heaven because we are all His children. To please God requires that we love one another as He has loved us (see John 13:34).

The alternative to at-one-ment with one's best self is selfishness, an unhealthy focus on self. We are selfish primarily because we lack the knowledge of who and whose we really are. In such a selfish state we cannot possibly build bonds of Zion with others. Brother Swain makes this point. "The selfish person isn't the one who loves himself; it is the one who has negative feelings about himself, who is self-centered, who is focusing on himself, trying to overcome his misgivings about himself. One who is at war with himself does not have peace of mind; he has inner conflict. If we can help a child develop self-love, then he is likely to be free from inner conflict and free to give kindness and love to others."[6]

At-one-ment with God and Others

Those who know who they are and live in harmony with God and His laws also live in harmony and joy with each other. Mormon explained that because of the love of God that dwelled in the hearts of the people, "there were no envyings, nor strifes, nor tumults, nor whoredoms, nor lyings, nor murders, nor any manner of lasciviousness; and surely there could not be a happier people among all the people who had been created by the hand of God" (4 Nephi 1:15–16).

At-one-ment with God requires that we strive for at-one-ment with those He loves. John learned this truth as he was returning home from his work at the office on a cold winter day. As John was pulling into his driveway, he remembered he had forgotten to pick up their youngest daughter from an activity. He realized she was still waiting for him and probably cold. He also knew that his relationship with Amy would suffer if he failed to care for and collect their daughter. So as quickly and quietly as possible, he backed out of his driveway and sought for and brought home their young (and cold) daughter.

Applying John's experience to ourselves, could we possibly hope for harmony with God if we forget or neglect our responsibility for the well-being of His children? Thus, an essential requirement for harmony with God is harmony with others—whenever possible without sacrificing at-one-ment with our best selves and God.

The first and great commandment is to become one with God through connections of love. However, to love God requires that we also love those He loves. Thus, the second great commandment is "to love our neighbor as ourselves."

Consider the Savior's teachings requiring that we be one with others if we are to be one with Him. He taught, "Therefore, if ye shall come unto me, or shall desire to come unto me, and rememberest that thy brother hath aught against thee—go thy way unto thy brother, and first be reconciled to thy brother, and then come unto me with full purpose of heart, and I will receive you" (3 Nephi 12:23–24). In First John we read about the at-one-ment between God and man. "If a man say, I love God, and hateth his brother, he is a liar: for he that loveth not his brother whom he hath seen, how can he love God whom he hath not seen? And this commandment have we from him. That he who loveth God love his brother also" (1 John 4:20–21).

The Prophet Joseph Smith taught regarding the at-one-ment between man and God, "The nearer we get to our Heavenly Father, the more we are disposed to look with compassion on perishing souls; we feel that we want to take them upon our shoulders, and cast their sins behind our backs. My talk is intended for all this society; if you would have God have mercy on you, have mercy on one another."[7]

I remember a particular attraction in an amusement park I visited. It was a merry-go-round that was shaped like a large inverted cone made of stainless steel. It was constructed using ball bearings that allowed the merry-go-round to spin at great speeds. The challenge and the thrill for the riders was to stay at the middle of the merry-go-round as it generated significant centrifugal force—a power that most often sent riders to its edge. The only safety was near the center. But even if you were near the center, you couldn't resist the centrifugal force and would be swept away unless you held on to someone else opposite you and also near the center of the merry-go-round. One person alone could never resist being pulled to the outer edge of the merry-go-round.

The analogy is that God is at the center of our world. We can only stay in His presence if we hold on to each other by serving and helping others to resist the forces of the world that would pull them away from Him. Only by holding on and helping others stay near Him are we able to overcome the forces of the world.

The Three Nephites, disciples chosen by Christ in the New World, desired to tarry so they could bless mankind. This request, however, meant postponing their reunion with the Savor in His kingdom. Their willingness to postpone their reunion with the Savior in order to bless their brethren illustrates the higher principle of at-one-ment. We become one with the Savior when we love and serve those He loves.

I learned about the need to be one with others from my mother. When Bonnie and I were first married we enrolled in graduate school at the University of Illinois. Our income was limited to my fellowship and occasional income from Bonnie's substitute teaching. When Ryan was born, our budget was stretched thin because of additional expenses. At the time, Bonnie was teaching in the Primary held on a week-day. Naomi Fitzgerald offered to watch Ryan while Bonnie was at Primary. Then every week when Bonnie and I came to pick up our son, Paul and Naomi Fitzgerald invited us to stay for dinner. They not only provided us a wonderful meal, they also provided us warm friendship and encouragement to pursue our educational goals.

Several years later and established in our profession, we agreed to host a student from another country for a year. Bonnie and I agreed to this arrangement because the student's mother was concerned about the quality of the school her son attended and his lack of academic progress. We enjoyed our year with our visiting student; however, one time during the year, he and I went on a walk together. I suggested the walk because there was a need to review his academic performance and his commitment to learn all that he could.

I asked him if he ever wondered why we agreed to host him for the year? He responded, "Well, I guess you just like me." I said, "Well we do like you, but at the time we agreed to host you, we hardly knew you. No," I said, "we agreed to host you not for anything you did, but because of what Paul and Naomi Fitzgerald did.

We cannot repay Paul and Naomi directly for their kindness. We can only thank them by helping someone else...that's the reason we agreed to host you."

We cannot repay the Savior for His infinite sacrifice, but we can be kind to and serve those He loves. Indeed, we have an obligation to do just that. This obligation to the Savior is contained in the commandment to "be one."

Internal At-one-ment and Integrity

The final object of our at-one-ment, and no less essential than our at-one-ment with God and others, is at-one-ment with our best selves—to be a person of integrity. The word *integrity* is derived from the Latin word for "untouched or entire." Thus integrity is the quality of being unimpaired, possessing unity, or wholeness. A person of integrity is who he or she appears to be. A person of integrity is guided by a core set of principles rather than by the values of his or her present company. Finally, a person of integrity has the same set of values yesterday, today, and tomorrow.

We are what we think about, desire, envision, and do. When these are in agreement and constant in the same cause, we are persons of integrity. However, when one of these is in conflict with the others or is inconstant in a cause, we lack integrity. The scribes and Pharisees of Christ's day lacked integrity because they tried to appear to be something they were not. The Savior condemned these hypocrites for their lack of integrity and compared them to "whited sepulchres"—beautiful on the outside but full of dead men's bones on the inside (see Matthew 23:27).

Integrity does not change its principles when its present company changes. Once, the Apostle Peter lacked integrity because he altered his allegiance. In the company of the Savior, Peter declared, "Though all men shall be offended because of thee, yet will I never be offended" (Matthew 26:33). Then when his company and the cost of discipleship changed, Peter denied his connection to the Savior declaring, "I know not the man" (Matthew 26:74).

President Hinckley has said, "In all this world there is no substitute for personal integrity. It includes honor. It includes performance. It includes keeping one's word. It includes doing what is right regardless of the circumstances."[8]

Later, Peter modeled the integrity President Hinckley described—unwavering in his commitment to follow the Savior, regardless of the crowd or the consequences. Before the Sadducees who commanded that neither he nor John speak at all nor teach in the name of Jesus, Peter answered, "Whether it be right in the sight of God to hearken unto you more than unto God, judge ye. For we cannot, but speak the things which we have seen and heard" (Acts 4:18–20).

Integrity is constant, and once it puts its hand to the plow, it does not look back nor recalculate the cost of discipleship. President Karl G. Maeser once described this aspect of integrity, honor. He said, "I have been asked what I mean by word of honor. I will tell you. Place me behind prison walls—walls of stone ever so high, ever so thick, reaching ever so far into the ground—there is a possibility that in some way or another I may be able to escape; but stand me on the floor and draw a chalk line around me and have me give my word of honor never to cross it. Can I get out of that circle? No, never! I'd die first!"[9]

One difference between Laman and Lemuel and Nephi and Sam was that Nephi and Sam possessed integrity. They were constant in the cause. In contrast, on occasion Laman and Lemuel repented and acquired integrity, usually after they were rebuked by an angel. But, then they changed their minds and were soon murmuring again about the cuisine and other discomforts as they followed Lehi reluctantly on the trail to the promised land.

God is the same yesterday, today, and tomorrow, and so are those who truly possess integrity. Joseph Smith's integrity led him to remain constant in his declaration of the truths revealed from heaven even when he was persecuted for doing so. He declared, "Why does the world think to make me deny what I have actually seen? For I had seen a vision; I knew it, and I knew that God knew it, and I could not deny it" (JSH 1:25).

We gain integrity through the process of repentance and conversion. We become converted when we possess consistent and constant thoughts, visions, desires, and deeds. Before Peter denied his discipleship, the Savior declared, "when thou art converted, strengthen thy brethren" (Luke 22:32).

Elder Bruce R. McConkie explained, "In the full gospel sense, however, conversion is more—far more—than merely changing one's belief from that which is false to that which is true; it is more than the acceptance of the verity of gospel truths, than the acquirement of a testimony. To convert is to change from one status to another, and gospel conversion consists in the transformation of man from his fallen and carnal state to a state of saintliness. A convert is one who…has been born again: where once he was spiritually dead, he has been regenerated to a state of spiritual life…he changes his whole way of life, and the nature and structure of his very being is quickened and changed by the power of the Holy Ghost."[10]

A poem by Edward Sanford Martin describes the condition of those who lack integrity:

> Within my earthly temple there's a crowd;
> There's one of us that's humble, one that's proud,
> There's one that's broken-hearted for his sins,
> There's one that unrepentant sits and grins;
> There's one that loves his neighbor as himself,
> And one that cares for naught, but fame and [s]elf.
> From much corroding care I should be free
> If I could once determine which is me.[11]

Ralph Waldo Emerson described how we change when we finally determine who we are. "Every man takes care that his neighbor shall not cheat him. But a day comes when he begins to care that he [does] not cheat his neighbor. Then all goes well. He has changed his market-cart into a chariot of the sun."[12]

Amy's Class

The class began as Amy anticipated, with busy twelve- and thirteen-year-old Beehive girls chatting away and whispering even though they had no real secrets to share. Amy called for their attention, and they reluctantly came to order. Then Amy introduced her lesson. "Today we will discuss the importance of unity, unity that can and should exist between us and that can even exist between enemy soldiers." Then she read the account of Brother Lauitzen.

"Now let me ask you a question," Amy queried. "The Lord wants us to be united or one. So who are the most important people in your lives, the ones with whom you most want to be one?" It was an easy question and the girls replied in unison, "Our parents!" Then Amy noticed Diana. She was sitting alone and fighting to hold back her tears. Amy caught her breath and silently berated herself. *How could I have been so insensitive?*

Diana's parents, previously both active members of their ward, were in the middle of a divorce. Diana's dad had already moved out and was living in an apartment across town. The bishop stressed to the members of the ward that they should be supportive of the family and should not take sides. But, that was easier said than done for some. Sometimes, some members of the Beehive class, likely influenced by their parents, talked about Diana and her parents' divorce—in whispers when they didn't think Diana could hear or notice. But she could usually guess that they were talking about her family and their gossip made her wonder if she really belonged with her friends anymore. Sometimes the pain of her parents' separation led Diana to miss church. Other times she wondered how she could continue without both parents at home and how God could let such a tragedy happen.

Oh! Amy exclaimed inwardly, *If anyone wanted a lesson on the importance of at-one-ment between parents, they only needed to attend this class and see broken-hearted Diana.*

Conclusions

The commandment to be one has at least three objects—God, others, and one's best self. When we have achieved at-one-ment with God, we gain eternal life and are saved. When we gain at-one-ment with others, we become part of a Zion community. And when we achieve at-one-ment with our best selves, we are converted into people of integrity. These three at-one-ments happen together or not at all.

The people who followed Enoch were blessed with a remarkable condition of at-one-ment with each other. "And the Lord called his people ZION, because they were of one heart and one mind, and dwelt in righteousness; and there were no poor among them" (Moses 7:18). Among these people there was agreement, charity, and equality that resulted from letting the will of God become their own.

Those who listened to King Benjamin and covenanted to obey God's commandments were converted into persons of integrity. This conversion was described as follows: "And they all cried with one voice, saying: Yea, we believe all the words which thou hast spoken unto us; and also, we know of their surety and truth, because of the Spirit of the Lord Omnipotent, which has wrought a mighty change in us, or in our hearts, that we have no more disposition to do evil, but to do good continually" (Mosiah 5:2).

Finally, as we earn our citizenship in Zion by living lives of integrity and service to others, we experience a change in our relationship with God. At first our faith leads us to obey without a perfect knowledge, we become His servants (see D&C 1:6). Then as we learn to obey, and let His will become our own, He calls us His friend (see D&C 84:77). And finally as His thoughts, desires, deeds, and visions become our own, we become His sons or daughters (see D&C 11:30) and gain eternal life, the greatest of all the gifts of God (see D&C 6:13).

NOTES

1. Russell M. Nelson, "Joy Cometh in the Morning" *Ensign,* November 1986, 67.

2. Quoted by Spencer W. Kimball, in Albert L. Zobell, Jr., *Storyteller's Scrapbook,* (1948), 112–113.

3. Edgar Rice Burroughs, *Tarzan of the Apes,* (1912).

4. Neal A. Maxwell, "The Tugs and Pulls of the World," *Ensign,* November 2000, 35.

5. "I Am a Child of God," *Hymns of The Church of Jesus Christ of Latter-day Saints*, no. 301.

6. Clark Swain, "The Meaning of Love," *Ensign,* March 1972, 26.

7. *Teachings of the Prophet Joseph Smith,* sel. Joseph Fielding Smith (1976), 241.

8. *Teachings of Gordon B. Hinckley,* (1997), 270.

9. *Vital Quotations*, comp. Emerson Roy West, (1968), 167.

10. Quoted by Daniel H. Ludlow, "I Have a Question," *Ensign,* December 1974, 26–27.

11. "My Name Is Legion," in Obert C. Tanner, *Christ's Ideals for Living,* (1955), 118.

12. *The Complete Writings of Ralph Waldo Emerson,* (1929), 585.

Chapter Four

LEADING TO AT-ONE-MENT

And Jesus, walking by the sea of Galilee, saw two
brethren, Simon called Peter, and Andrew his brother,
casting a net into the sea: for they were fishers.
And he saith unto them, Follow me, and
I will make you fishers of men.

—Matthew 4:18–19

格 १०

John tried to settle inconspicuously into a pew near the rear of the chapel. He had arrived nearly ten minutes late to stake priesthood meeting and the stake president had just opened the meeting and was introducing the theme for the evening. John enjoyed President Strong's talks because they always seemed to contain a message especially designed for him.

President Strong began by welcoming and thanking the brethren for their attendance at the priesthood leadership meeting. Then he asked, "Why do we need a leadership meeting?" John thought to himself, *Good question.* Then President Strong answered his own question. "The reason is because we are all leaders…we all have some influence on someone to do something…and we need to be sure we are leading others to Christ." Then President Strong paused, took off his glasses and looked at the audience. John imagined he was looking directly at him. "Brethren, we can do better, much better, in leading our families and others back to Christ." Then with almost a pleading tone he continued. "Some of your families are suffering because we are not leading in the way Christ would lead. For this reason, tonight's meeting is focused on becoming a Christlike leader."

President Strong's comments made John uncomfortable. He began to rationalize. *I'm doing okay, I think.* But then he remembered his confrontation with his ten-year-old son Mark who had failed in one of his household duties. Instead of taking the trash to the garbage can, Mark left it in the garage—he was in a hurry and besides it was Saturday morning and his cousins were visiting.

John felt a pang of guilt sweep over him. He had criticized and humiliated Mark in front of everyone. He remembered the hurt in Mark's eyes and the separation he felt between them. *Is this the way Christ would lead?* The question seemed to come out of nowhere.

John listened intently to what followed. President Strong then asked, "What are the qualities that we must seek for to become a Christlike leader?" John took out his pen and paper and began to record President Strong's instructions on how to become a Christlike leader.

What Is Leadership? What Makes a Great Leader?

Leadership is the ability to capacitate and motivate others to physical, emotional, and mental action. Book of Mormon military leader, Chief Captain Moroni, and World War II statesman, Winston Churchill, exemplified great leadership because they capacitated and motivated others to great acts requiring significant sacrifices.

During a critical time for the Nephites when internal dissent threatened their society, Chief Captain Moroni called his people to enter into a covenant to maintain their liberty. In response, the people "came running together with their armor girded about their loins" (Alma 46:21). During a critical time in the world's history when Nazi tyranny threatened the world, Winston Churchill "was able with his stirring speeches to will British courage into existence by getting his compatriots to see themselves in the same, almost mythic terms in which he saw them.... In the end, it changed the outcome of the war."[1]

The world needs good and great leaders because when the wicked rule, the people mourn; when the righteous rule, the people prosper. Thus, the Lord commanded that "honest men and wise men should be sought for diligently" (D&C 98:8–10) and that He, the Lord, would select His rulers from among His noble and great children (see Abraham 3:22–23). The Church emphasizes the importance of good and great leaders today by attending to their training—in worldwide *leadership* training meetings conducted by the First Presidency and Quorum of the Twelve, stake priesthood *leadership* meetings, and Saturday evening *leadership* meetings. In the home, members are encouraged to teach Christlike leadership principles in family home evenings and family councils.

Society signals the importance of leaders by assigning to them titles of respect such as chief, general, admiral, commander, president, executive, and director. Often, organizations define themselves by their leadership structure, and some persons assess their own importance and that of others by their leadership assignments. History honors great leaders by recording their deeds in music and the written word, remembering them with statues and paintings, placing their names on important buildings, and discussing their lives in special seminars. We may never be featured in large corporate organizational charts, occupy pages in a history book, or even have our likeness displayed on a monument; nevertheless, we are all leaders because we are all leading someone, somewhere, through our personal influence, to do something.

Parents lead their children to adulthood. The salesperson leads his customer to the sale. The doctor leads her patient to a treatment. And missionaries lead their investigators to Christ and conversion. Thus, our choice is not whether or not to be leaders, but what kind of leaders we will be. Will we lead people to mourn or to prosper? Whatever will be our influence, the Lord holds us responsible.

President David O'McKay taught, "There is one responsibility that no one can evade. That is the effect of one's personal influence."[2] To prepare to be great and good leaders, we should study and learn from the one perfect leader, Jesus Christ. Spencer W. Kimball taught, "Those individuals whom we most love, admire, and respect as leaders of the human family are so regarded by us precisely because they embody, in many ways, the qualities that Jesus had in this life and in his leadership."[3]

To become Christlike leaders, we must adopt the mission to bring souls to God and eternal life, and to do this we must become more like Christ. What distinguishes Christlike leaders from other great leaders? It is their at-one-ment with God whom they follow, their at-one-ment with their best selves reflected by their vision of who they are and where they are to lead, and their at-one-ment with those being led. Achieving these dimensions of at-one-ment will lead us to be more like the greatest of all leaders, Jesus Christ, who under the most difficult circumstances, realized the greatest of all visions—to lead mankind to His Father and eternal life.

Christlike Leaders and Followers

Christlike leaders are first, Christlike followers. The Savior exemplified this leadership requirement in the beginning when He distinguished Himself from Satan by His willingness to follow Heavenly Father's plan. And when the fate of humankind depended on the Savior's discipleship, and while weighed down by the sins and sufferings of the world, Christ, the Lamb of God, declared His determination to follow. "Father, if thou be willing, remove this cup from me: nevertheless not my will, but thine, be done" (Luke 22:42).

Nephi, a great prophet-leader, was also a perfect follower. When asked to return to Jerusalem and obtain the plates, he responded, "I will go and do the things which the Lord hath commanded, for I know that the Lord giveth no commandments unto the children of men, save he shall prepare a way for them that they may accomplish the thing which he commandeth them" (1 Nephi 3:7).

The alternative to following God is to follow others. Henry D. Taylor described what happens when our loyalty to an individual exceeds our loyalty to God. Lyman Wright was a devoted friend and associate of the Prophet Joseph Smith, and when the Prophet was unjustly placed in the dungeon at Liberty Jail, Wright with other close friends accompanied Joseph. Following the Prophet's martyrdom, Wright declared, "The only man who can handle me is dead." He became rebellious and unmanageable and refused to follow the leadership of Brigham Young and the Twelve. Finally he led a group of his followers to Texas, where he sank into obscurity and oblivion. Why? Because his loyalty to a dead prophet was greater than his loyalty to God and his living prophet.[4]

Great leaders recognize their need to follow God and to be guided by His wisdom, to see His vision, to love with His love, and to act in His power. Abraham Lincoln reflected this humble dependence on God when he wrote, "I have been driven many times upon my knees by the overwhelming conviction that I had nowhere else to go. My own wisdom and that of all about me seemed insufficient for that day."[5]

No one can be a great leader who is not also a great follower of our Heavenly Father. The Savior, who was the one perfect leader, was also the one perfect follower of His Father. As a result,

He could describe Himself as both the Good Shepherd (see John 10:11) and also the Lamb of God (see John 1:29). From the Savior we learn that all of us sometimes should be lambs that follow a good shepherd and sometimes good shepherds that lead lambs. If we are unwilling to be lambs that follow, it is unlikely that we can ever become skilled shepherds who lead.

Christlike Leaders and Integrity

Christlike leaders have integrity reflected by a consistency between what they create spiritually, desire, believe, and do. This internal unity defeats traitorous doubts that attempt to discourage us from acting. William Shakespeare eloquently penned, "Our doubts are traitors, and make us lose the good we oft might win by fearing to attempt."[6] Consider each dimension of our integrity and what they contribute to leadership.

Spiritual Creations

A vision is a spiritual creation produced by one's imagination and inspiration. Unless we have a spiritual creation, we have no place to live out our lives. Visions can be mighty or meek, but we can only truly worship God with a mighty vision that leads us to vanquish our doubts and fears, and to act. George Bernard Shaw wrote, "Some look at things that are, and ask why? I dream of things that never were and ask why not?"[7]

All great leaders have at least two kinds of visions—who they are and where they are to lead. These two visions are related. The vision leaders have of who they are determines their vision of where they are to lead. Having a vision that we are children of divinity and that our destiny is to become like our Father in Heaven prepares us to be great leaders. John the Beloved confirms this vision, "Beloved, now are we the sons of God, and it doth not yet appear what we shall be: but we know that, when he shall appear, we shall be like him; for we shall see him as he is" (1 John 3:2).

Timid souls, unaware of their capacities, are unlikely to lead others to great deeds. Only leaders who see themselves as strong, capable, and connected to divinity dare to dream mighty visions. What made the Savior the greatest of all leaders was His vision of Himself as the Divine Son of God. When tempted, His divine denouncement of Satan was, "Thou shalt not tempt the Lord thy God" (Luke 4:12), and when doubted by disbelieving countrymen He prophetically proclaimed, "Before Abraham was, I am" (John 8:58).

Once great leaders have a vision of who they are, they dare dream mighty visions of how, where, and when they are to lead. Joseph Smith was given a vision in the Sacred Grove in which he saw that through him the true Church of Jesus Christ would be restored. Brigham Young climbed Ensign Peak and saw his vision of how to settle the Lord's people. Jacob taught in the temple, only after he received "his errand from the Lord" (Jacob 1:17). Moses saw in vision the promised land of Canaan where he was to lead the Israelites. Lehi and Nephi likewise were shown visions of the tree of life where they were to gather their families.

In our day and time, temples can become for us the sacred grove or the mountain of revelation where we see ourselves as who we really are and where we are to lead. Elder David B. Haight taught, "Come to the temples worthily and regularly. Not only do you bless those who are deceased, but you may freely partake of the promised personal revelation that may bless your life with power, knowledge, light, beauty, and truth from on high, which will guide you and your posterity to eternal life."[8]

President Strong paused in his presentation and once he had everyone's attention, he continued. "Now brethren, gaining a vision of who we are and where we are to lead is not merely an exercise in positive thinking, we must do more than believe to achieve Christ-like results. We must adopt God's vision, not our own or those of others. When our vision of how to lead is the same as His, our weaknesses will be transformed into strengths."

Great Desires

Great visions can only be realized by those willing to make great sacrifices. Great visions have one common element—they require a journey beyond the well worn path. And the travel beyond the comfortable always requires sacrifice. And only those leaders who passionately desire to realize their vision are willing to make the sacrifices their visions require.

Believable Beliefs

Great leaders believe firmly that what they created spiritually in their visions and what they passionately desire can be realized through planning, preparation, and sacrifice. One preventable problem sometimes made by weak leaders is to set impressive, unrealistic goals that bruise the beliefs of those required to achieve them. Belief is strengthened when leaders set realistic goals consistent with their responsibilities.

Another way great leaders increase the belief that their goals can be achieved is by planning for their realization. Indeed, a vision without a plan remains a dream. Thus, all great leaders plan. Planning moves one's spiritual creation down the road to a realized result. A proper plan describes what resources will be necessary and how they will be obtained and organized to realize the leader's vision. A proper plan sets priorities, establishes connections, and assigns responsibilities.

In the premortal council, our Father in Heaven presented not only the goal of our immortality and eternal life, but also His plan of happiness for reaching this goal. The Savior connected goal setting and planning when he taught, "For which of you, intending to build a tower, sitteth not down first, and counteth the cost, whether he have sufficient to finish it?" (Luke 14: 28). Plans become workable when persons accept assignments to assure its success. To assure the success of the Father's plan of happiness, Christ accepted the assignment of becoming our Savior which the plan required.

Doing

Some wise pundit proclaimed that after all is said and done, there is more said than done. Not so with great leaders—great leaders act. Their first action is to prepare to realize their plan. President Gordon B. Hinckley declared, "In missionary work, as in all else, preparation precedes power."[9] Great leaders realize that if they are prepared, they shall not fear nor fail (see D&C 38:30).

The Savior went to the desert for forty days to prepare His thoughts and desires prior to performing the great deeds of His ministry. Joseph Smith prepared himself to do great deeds by learning true doctrines in the process of translating the Book of Mormon. Successful missionaries have spent their lives strengthening their testimonies through prayer, study, and service.

But success requires more than preparation. One of the most interesting and controversial personalities of the Civil War was Union General George B. McClellan. He was a great organizer, he prepared well, and he was loved and admired by his men. Yet, he was reluctant to fight. Before the Civil War battle of Antietam, Union soldiers found Confederate General Robert E. Lee's battle plans and turned them over to General McClellan, providing him with a significant advantage. However, General McClellan failed to act decisively on his knowledge and, as a result, failed to gain the victory over the numerically inferior Confederate armies. General McClellan's failure to act, many claim, prolonged the Civil War.

In contrast, successful leaders act. Or in the words of President Ezra Taft Benson, successful missionary leaders work. He taught,

"One of the greatest secrets of missionary work is work! If a missionary works, he will get the Spirit; if he gets the Spirit, he will teach by the Spirit; and if he teaches by the Spirit, he will touch the hearts of the people and he will be happy. There will be no homesickness, no worrying about families, for [he will have] all [his] time and talents and interest…centered on the work of the ministry. Work, work, work—there is no satisfactory substitute, especially in missionary work." [10]

Christlike Leaders Love Those They Lead

Christlike leaders fuel their vision, desires, beliefs, and deeds by a love of others. Indeed, what makes great leaders into Christlike leaders is that they love those they lead. This love provides those being led the assurance that their leaders care about their condition and will lead them whenever possible "beside the still waters." While other virtues such as faith and hope are essential, charity is the greatest of all because our greatest need is for charity or love. Victor Hugo wrote that "the supreme happiness of life is the conviction that we are loved.[11] The Savior's leadership was powered by His love and the greatest example of this love was His willingness to lay down His life to save all of God's children. Likewise, the scriptures speak of our Heavenly Father's love for us. "For God so loved the world, that he gave his only begotten Son, that whosoever believeth in him should not perish, but have everlasting life" (John 3:16).

Leaders who love those they lead want them to achieve greatness. Self absorbed, underachieving leaders want those they lead to be at-one with their own level of mediocrity. Elder Neal A. Maxwell taught, "One wonders if the tolerance of unnecessary mediocrity in others isn't at some deep level of consciousness, a way of protecting ourselves or excusing ourselves for our own personal mediocrity. In human relationships there are too many tacit, silent deals in which one person agrees not to demand full measure, if the other person will agree to mediocrity when excellence may be possible."[12]

A love for those they lead fuels leaders with strong desires and converts them from hirelings to good shepherds. Leaders may gain followers through intimidation, bribes, or threats. While these methods may produce conformity for a moment, they can never create the unifying connections required for long term success. Furthermore, this type of leadership is condemned by the Lord because it prevents us from drawing on the powers of heaven (see D&C 121:36–37). Only loving leadership has the power to lift us and others to greatness.

The scriptures repeatedly remind us that Christlike leaders love. "Press forward with steadfastness in Christ, having love of God and all men" (2 Nephi 31:20). "Pray that you may be filled with this love" (Moroni 7:48). "We love him because he first loved us" (1 John 4:19). Then filled with a love for others, we serve. The Savior declared, "But he that is greatest among you shall be your servant" (Matthew 23:11).

Christlike Leaders Develop Christlike Leadership in Those They Lead

Great leaders are at-one with those they lead because they are guided by two important principles. First, they know that no significant vision can be realized without the help of others; and second, they know that all Christlike visions require the growth and development of those being led. Therefore, whatever else the Christlike leader seeks to achieve, his primary project is the development of Christlike leadership among those he or she leads. It is significant that Christ spent so much of His ministry preparing His chosen Twelve Apostles to lead. This important focus of Christlike leaders was summarized poetically by President Boyd K. Packer who adapted a poem by Edwin Markham:

We are all blind, until we see
That in the [universal] plan
Nothing is worth the making if
It does not make the man.

Why build these [buildings] glorious,
If man unbuilded goes?
In vain we build the [world], unless
The builder also grows.[13]

One way leaders develop the leadership of those they lead is by treating them as though they already had acquired greatness. For example, one time Lehi failed to lead and complained against the Lord. Noble Nephi helped restore his father's leadership by recognizing him as his father-prophet and by appealing to him to obtain a revelation from the Lord to resolve their hunger crisis (see 1 Nephi 16:23).

Another way that leaders lead their followers to greatness is by inspiring them with important assignments. In the case of Moroni, it was recorded that during a critical battle between the Nephites and Lamanites, "the men of Moroni saw the fierceness and the anger of the Lamanites, [and] they were about to shrink and flee from them. And Moroni, perceiving their intent, sent forth and inspired their hearts with these thoughts—yea, the thoughts of their lands, their liberty, yea their freedom from bondage. And it came to pass that they turned upon the Lamanites, and they cried with one voice unto the Lord their God, for their liberty and their freedom from bondage. And they began to stand against the Lamanites with power" (Alma 43:48–50).

Great leaders recognize that to develop leadership, those being led must be given opportunities to exercise their agency. Therefore, great leaders empower others with the privilege of making their own choices. Joseph Smith, when asked how he governed his people, responded, "I teach them correct principles and they govern themselves" (Journal of Discourses 10:57).

Finally, great leaders lead others to become great leaders by being their example. The Savior taught, "Come, follow me!" (Luke 18:22). "Do the things which ye have seen me do" (2 Nephi 31:12). He asked the Nephites, "Therefore, what manner of men ought ye to be?" And He answered, "Verily I say unto you, even as I am" (3 Nephi 27:27).

President Strong concluded. "Brethren, let us be examples to our families. Let them look to us for an example to follow. Our greatest leadership challenge and opportunity is within our own homes—simply because home is where we so often treat the ones we love the most the worst. Let us do better." President Strong then bore his powerful testimony that the Lord needs his priesthood to become great leaders, especially in their homes. John knew he needed to be better.

Measures of Christlike Leadership

Christlike leaders are accountable for the influence they have on others. So we ask, what are the measures of Christlike leadership?

Christlike Leaders Attract Christlike Followers

The first measure of a leader is the kind of people attracted to the leader's cause. "For intelligence cleaveth unto intelligence; wisdom receiveth wisdom; truth embraceth truth; virtue loveth virtue; light cleaveth unto light; mercy hath compassion on mercy and claimeth her own; justice continueth its course and claimeth its own..." (D&C 88:40). Christlike followers are attracted to Christlike leaders and take the Holy Ghost as their guide (see Acts 1:16). The world follows those who are wise in their own eyes and understanding (see 1 Corinthians 2:14).

Christlike Leaders Inspire Christlike Followers to Make Great Sacrifices for Their Cause

Christlike leaders inspire Christlike followers to make great sacrifices because of the importance of the cause—to bring souls to Christ. President Ezra Taft Benson described the sacrifices of those who followed the Savior and their sacrifices. The "rugged, able men whom He called to be His Apostles gave up prosperous business careers to follow Him. Many of His delegated missionaries traveled without purse or scrip. Men suffered great hardships in carrying out His instructions. Some of them died cruel deaths in His service. But His delegated disciples went forth into the world bold as lions through His charge. They accomplished things they had never dreamed of. No leader ever motivated men and women as did He."[14]

Joseph Smith revealed that "a religion that does not require the sacrifice of all things never has power sufficient to produce the faith necessary unto life and salvation."[15]

Christlike Leaders Lead Christlike Followers to Success

The third measure of a leader's success is what their followers become. Wicked Lamanite leaders such as Amalakiah and Ammoron led their followers to destruction. In contrast, those who followed Chief Captain Moroni such as Teancum, Lehi, Antipus, and Helaman became great generals like their leader, Moroni.

"Teancum...had been a man who had fought valiantly for his country, yea, a true friend to liberty; and he had suffered very many exceedingly sore afflictions" (Alma 62:37). "Lehi was a man who had been with Moroni in the more part of all his battles; and he was a man like unto Moroni, and they rejoiced in each other's safety; yea, they were beloved by each other and also beloved by all the people of Nephi" (Alma 53:2). Antipus demonstrated his greatness by leading his men to extraordinary exertions to save Helaman and his army of stripling warriors (see Alma 56:38). Helaman, chosen by the 2000 stripling warriors to be their leader, inspired his young sons to return from safety to save the army of Antipus and to fight without fear (see Alma 53:19; Alma 56:45–47).

Christlike Leadership Is Measured by the Leader's Legacy

Great leaders leave a legacy. The Lord instructed Lehi to return to Jerusalem to obtain the plates so they would not forget the lesson taught by former leaders. And when the Savior came to the Nephites He commanded them to write down the great teachings of their prophets and to remember His teachings. We are instructed to keep journals to record the things that we have learned, so that having learned important lessons we can avoid many mistakes. Therefore, leaders leave instructions for those who will come later; they plan for their leadership to continue after they have left.

Christlike Leadership Is Measured by the At-One-Ment between Leaders and Those They Lead

The Savior prayed that His disciples would be "one" so that the world might know that He had sent them (see John 17:21). Likewise great leaders lead in such a way that competition and pride are not allowed to destroy the unity of those being led. The unity created by Christlike leaders prevents selfish squabbles that waste precious synergy and undo achievements won by working together. This at-one-ment is made possible because the leaders and those being led love one another, and this love leads them to seek for the well-being of each other.

Christlike Leadership Is Measured by What the Leader Gave

When we talk about great leaders, we often mention their qualities that allowed them to remain steadfast and firm in leading others to their vision. Still, the most distinguishing characteristic of Christ's leadership and its alternative is giving versus getting.

World-centered leadership is about getting. Christlike leadership is about giving. World-centered leadership is about acting selfishly. Christlike leadership is about acting charitably. World-centered leaders measure their success by their accumulated wealth and power. Christlike leaders measure their success by the achievements of those they serve. Finally, world-centered leaders win contests. Christlike leaders win souls for Christ, including their own.

ℭℜ ℰℴ

Mark was already in bed when John returned home from priesthood leadership meeting. John stepped quietly into his room and sat on his bed. Mark was sleeping soundly, but roused when he felt his dad tousle his hair. "Hi Dad," Mark mumbled. "Mark," John began, "I want to apologize for what I did last Saturday. That was wrong for me to chew you out in front of everyone. I'm sorry and I want to do much better…to be more like the kind of dad the Savior wants me to be." Mark sleepily mouthed the words, "That's okay Dad," and was asleep. At that moment John felt a sense of deep love for his son and wondered if that was similar, in some small way, to how God felt about him.

Notes

1. Peter McGrath, "The Battle of Britain, 50 Years Ago." *Newsweek*, August 20, 1990, 56.

2. Quoted by Thomas S. Monson, "Your Personal Influence," *Ensign,* May 2004, 20.

3. Spencer W. Kimball, "Jesus: The Perfect Leader," From an address delivered to the Young Presidents organization, Sun Valley, Idaho, 15 January 1977.

4. Henry Taylor, Conference Report, April 1967, 39.

5. *Lincoln Observed: The Civil War Dispatches of Noah Brooks,* edited by Michael Burlingame. Johns Hopkins University Press, Baltimore, (1998), 210.

6. William Shakespeare, *Measure for Measure*, act 1, scene 4.

7. George Bernard Shaw, "Back to Methuselah," act 1, *Selected Plays with Prefaces,* vol. 2, (1949), 7.

8. David B. Haight, "Rejoice in the Blessings of the Temple," *Ensign*, December 2002, 63

9. Quoted by Robert L. Backman, "Called To Serve," *Ensign*, November 1987, 60.

10. *The Teachings of Ezra Taft Benson,* (1988), 200.

11   Victor Hugo, http://washingtonmo.com/words/01-10-23.htm.

12. Neal A. Maxwell, *A More Excellent Way*, (1967), 34.

13. Edwin Markham, "Man-Making," in *Masterpieces of Religious Verse,* ed. James Dalton Morrison, (1948), 419.

14. Ezra Taft Benson, *God, Family, Country*, (1974), 135.

15. Joseph Smith, *Lectures on Faith*, (reprinted 1985), 69.

Chapter Five

OUR SENSES OF AT-ONE-MENT

See that ye serve him with all of your heart,
might, mind, and strength

—D&C 4:2

CB EO

Amy and John stepped out the back door and began their familiar walk that took them past the neighborhood park where they frequently brought their children to play. It was sunset and they held hands as they strolled along. They loved these quiet times together that seemed to stir their feelings of love and admiration for each other—feelings they had felt so often in the early years of their marriage. Then a short way into their walk, they were brought back to the immediate present by the needs and activities of their four children.

Tomorrow was Saturday and like most Saturdays, it would begin with Frank and soccer. Frank was thirteen and their oldest. Frank, it seemed, needed to always be doing something physical, building, running, exercising. He was the star on their neighborhood soccer team partly because of his soccer skills, but mostly because of his aggressive approach toward the game. If there was a scramble for the ball, most likely Frank would be in the middle of it and emerge with the ball. If the game was close, Frank would take charge, directing his teammates. Frank was all about doing. School work, on the other hand, did not occupy a high position on his list of priorities.

In contrast, Mark, their ten-year-old, second son, loved to read. In so many ways he was the opposite of Frank. He loved to "think." He frequently surprised John and Amy because of his desire to be with adults and participate in their conversations. He could entertain himself for hours putting together a puzzle, reading a book, or asking questions that frequently began with the word *why*. In contrast to Frank who was often doing things before thinking and planning, Mark never acted impulsively—sometimes to the irritation of John and Amy. If one of their children was to become a studious scientist, Amy and John were convinced it would be Mark.

Samantha, their seven-year-old, was their social, butterfly. She was the most popular girl in her class. Everyone in her class, it seemed, wanted to claim Samantha as their "best" friend—and she was usually only too happy to oblige. For Sam, as everyone called her, having friends was the "best thing in the world." But needing and loving friends came at a cost. Sam could be especially hurt if she was left out of a game of dodgeball or not invited to a classmate's birthday party. On the other hand, no one enjoyed having family and friends visit more than Sam—and on these occasions she was full of hugs and kisses.

Finally, there was their four-year-old Heidi. Her most favorite thing in the world was to perform while her family was watching. Performances could include attempting a cartwheel, modeling clothes, showing off her most recent artwork, skipping, or imitating whatever she had observed her older sister do. However, her most distinguishing feature was her ability to create worlds in her mind. Castles, dragons, pet dogs and horses, and imaginary friends could all be part of Heidi's world.

Reflecting on all of their children, Amy exclaimed, "How can they all be so different?" John, attempting to respond to Amy's question, recalled having read that we were different in heaven. There, we were foreordained to our particular leadership responsibilities and endowed with different abilities and talents to do different things. There God assigned each of us to a particular time and place to be born "so we can learn the lessons we personally need and do the most good with our individual talents and personalities."[1]

Our Four Senses of At-one-ment

One explanation for the differences between Frank, Mark, Sam, and Heidi and between us is our differently developed senses of at-one-ment—differences that we may have possessed in the premortal world.

Man may sense at-one-ment when he reasons, feels emotion, envisions his possibilities, and experiences his body doing what his spirit directs. We can represent these senses of at-one-ment using the metaphors of the mind, heart, hands, and feet. Metaphors help us describe one concept efficiently by equating it to a second and different concept with similar traits. The Savior frequently used metaphors in His teachings. For example, He described His true disciples as "the salt of the earth," "lambs of His fold," and as "a light on the hill."

Because man's senses of at-one-ment reside in his soul—consisting of his body and spirit—there is a natural tendency for them to be at-one. What man thinks, feels, envisions, and does all tug on each other, seeking for harmony. Thus, activating any one of man's four senses of at-one-ment affects the others. What follows are descriptions of our senses of at-one-ment and how we strive to bring them into at-one-ment with each other.

Mind

With his mind, man has the capacity to sense what is and isn't, what was and wasn't, and what will and won't be. He utilizes his mind to connect questions and answers, cause and effect, the past with the present and future, and to distinguish between consistencies and contradictions. The mind also has the capacity to be blinded by disbelief or enlightened by the Spirit of the Lord (see D&C 110:1).

Clearly the Lord expects us to develop our mental capacity to sense at-one-ment. Gifted with intelligence, we are expected to study it out in our minds before asking God if what we are considering is right. After having studied the matter in our minds and having asked God if what we are considering is right, then the Lord will cause that "your bosom shall burn within you; therefore, you shall feel that it is right" (D&C 9:8). Elder Dallin H. Oaks taught that a "burning in the bosom" signifies a feeling of comfort and serenity—a sense of quiet confidence, comfort, and warmth, often identified by happiness, joy, and feelings of love.[2]

Heart

With his heart, man has the capacity to feel what others feel, to desire or disdain, to experience joy or sadness, and to sense the presence or absence of the Lord's Spirit. This sense allows him to understand more than can be understood by reason alone and feel what can't be seen. President Harold B. Lee observed this capacity of the heart when he taught, "When we understand more than we know with our minds, when we understand with our hearts, then we know that the Spirit of the Lord is working upon us."[3]

The Nephites enjoyed a heightened sense of understanding of the heart when they prayed during the Savior's visit and "their hearts were open and they did understand in their hearts the words which he prayed" (3 Nephi 19:33). Contrasting man's ability to understand in his heart with his power to reason with his mind, King Benjamin challenged his people. "Open your ears that ye may hear, and your hearts that ye may understand, and your minds that the mysteries of God may be unfolded to your view" (Mosiah 2:9).

One reason our understanding increases when we listen with our hearts is because of the heart's capacity to internalize the well-being of others. This ability produces an emotional state of at-one-ment or separation between us and others. Finally, while the Holy Ghost can speak to our minds and hearts, its dwelling place is in our hearts. The Lord revealed to Joseph Smith, "I will tell you in your mind and in your heart, by the Holy Ghost, which shall come upon you and which shall dwell in your heart" (D&C 8:2). Therefore, when the Holy Ghost communicates to us, His message often comes as a feeling.[4]

Hands

The metaphor of the hands describes man's capacity to create the future spiritually before the physical creation is attempted. It is with his hands that man signals and gives form to his visions. It is with his raised right hand in ward, stake, and general conferences that men and women express spiritually their willingness to support their leaders with their time and talents. Sometimes men and women visibly express the sorrow of their spirits by letting their hands hang down (see D&C 81:5).

It is with the extended hand that man offers and envisions friendship and agreement with others spiritually before being called upon to demonstrate their affection physically. It is with hands clapped together that man signals his appreciation of great achievements. It is with his hand raised to the square that men and women commit themselves to give honest testimony. It with his hands raised and pointing that man directs visually to others the way to go and who to follow. But in other times man gives substance to his visions with his hands as when the artist paints, the pianist performs, the architect draws, the potter shapes, and the mute and deaf communicate.

While man's spiritual creations are the result of his beliefs in what is possible and his desires for what he values, man's spiritual creations also reflect his strength of will. At one extreme, man's vision is a passing glance, a hurried view, or a fanciful dream. At the other extreme, man's vision is a fixed gaze, a determined plan to reach a goal regardless of the hazards. Thus, man's will or might is reflected in his hands and, in the end, produces the energy to do, not merely to dream.

Only the courageous envision bold dreams. Only those who love deeply envision service. Only those with confidence see mountains to climb. Understanding the connection between might and vision, it is interesting to note that in Hebrew, the most common word for hands is *yad,* which is also used metaphorically to mean power, strength, or might.[5]

Lawrence of Arabia described the difference between mighty and meek visions when he wrote, "All men dream, but not equally. Those who dream by night in the dusty recesses of their minds wake in the day to find that it was vanity, but dreamers of the day are [mighty] men, for they may act their dream with open eyes, to make it possible."[6] Worshipping with our might requires that our spiritual creation be dreamed in the day and then realized through mighty works.

Feet

Finally, the feet represent physical action—man exercising his strength and physical powers. With his feet man walks, obeys, serves, and pushes and pulls. The actions of our feet often express the summation of the potency of all of our other senses. After we have envisioned, believed, and desired, what do our feet do?

Man's feet also represent his contact with the world and that part of his being subject to the temptations of the natural man. This contact with the world and its natural-man's pull led the Lord to symbolically cleanse His disciples from the world's influence by washing their dirty feet. Interestingly enough, one of our most sacred purifying ordinances involves washing of the feet (see D&C 88:139).

But man's body, represented by his feet, when directed by the Spirit is capable of doing much good as the prophet Isaiah proclaims. "How beautiful upon the mountains are the *feet* of him that bringeth good tidings, that publisheth peace; that bringeth good tidings of good, that publisheth salvation; that saith unto Zion, Thy God reigneth!" (Isaiah 52:7; emphasis added).

Finally, the Lord commands us to "serve him with all [of our] heart, might, mind and strength, that [we] may stand blameless before God at the last day" (D&C 4:2). Using the metaphors of the mind, heart, hands, and feet, this command might be rephrased— believe in God with your mind, desire to serve Him with your heart, visualize His perfection and the possibility of your becoming like Him with your hands, and with all your strength walk in His ways.

Conscience and Our Four Senses of At-one-ment

Every man and woman is born with a conscience or the Light of Christ. Our conscience enlivens each of our four senses of at-one-ment. Operating through these senses, our conscience helps us distinguish between right and wrong—between those things that will bring us closer to God and help us become like Him and those things with the opposite effect. It is our conscience manifested through our senses of at-one-ment that makes it possible to exercise our moral agency and become accountable for our actions (see Moroni 7:16, 17; D&C 101:78). Like our other capacities, our moral agency can be strengthened through use or extinguished through neglect.[7]

Daniel Judd wrote about the influence of the Light of Christ on our hearts. "While the Spirit [Light] of Christ is manifest in a multitude of ways, perhaps the most personal and the most important of its dimensions is expressed as our conscience, or knowing "good from evil" (Moroni 7:16). "It is through our conscience that we first come to perceive the love of a Father in Heaven who does 'all things for the welfare and happiness of his people' (Helaman 12:2)."[8]

In the same article, Brother Judd noted that it was the Light of Christ that enlivened King Lamoni's mind to recognize the false teachings of his fathers (see Alma 18:5; Alma 19:6). It was also the Light of Christ that enabled Ammon to perceive the thoughts of the king (see Alma 18:16). It was the Light of Christ enhanced by the Holy Ghost that strengthened Ammon physically to defend King Lamoni's flocks against the robbers (see Alma 17:35–37; Alma 18:2). It was also the Light of Christ that empowered Nephi physically to burst the bands with which he had been bound by his brothers (see 1 Nephi 7:16–18).

President Joseph Fielding Smith wrote that the Light of Christ gave vision to all of the great inventors to see spiritually what could be created physically. "Those who make these discoveries are inspired of God or they would never make them. The Lord gave inspiration to Edison, to Franklin, to Morse, to Whitney and to all of the inventors and discoverers, and through their inspiration they obtained the necessary knowledge and were able to manufacture and invent as they have done for the benefit of the world. Without the Lord's inspiration they would have been just as helpless as the people were in other ages."[9] Similarly, it was the Light of Christ that inspired Columbus with a vision of discovery and later other Gentiles with a vision of religious freedom (see 1 Nephi 13:12–13).

The Interdependence of Man's Senses of At-one-ment

Our four senses of at-one-ment are like the four corners of a bedspread. Bedspreads are made up of different pieces of materials sewn together with needle and thread. When you pull on one corner of the bedspread, the other corners feel the stress and respond. So it is with our thoughts, feelings, visions, and deeds. A change in one of the four senses of at-one-ment has an effect on the others.

Suppose we have a weakness we wish to conquer. Rather than focus on the weakness, we may give attention to our strongest virtue. Doing so is like pulling on a corner of the bedspread opposite of where a wrinkle lurks. Suppose we have a desire we would like to change, but just can't seem to escape its grasp. Often the solution is to pull on the other side of our natures.

To do this, we may learn new lessons by reading the scriptures and witnessing the desire to do better. Or, we could envision a new mountain to climb and set personal goals—then notice how the focus of our desires shifts from dwelling in the valley to living in a mansion on the mountain peak. Or, practice a new skill or one that we want to improve—then feel our desire to develop companion skills expand. Express love to a friend and feel our desires to bless them swell. In so many different ways, as if by magic, the wrinkled desire disappears. Consider the evidence that our senses of at-one-ment are interdependent.

The Influence of the Man's Mind (Thoughts) on His Other Senses of At-one-ment

Ralph Waldo Emerson said, "A man is what he thinks about all day long." William James taught, "The greatest discovery of this generation is that human beings can alter their lives by altering their attitudes of mind."[10]

And from President David O. McKay, "What company do you keep when you are alone? What is your dominating train of thought? This to a great degree will shape your character.... The thought in your mind at this moment is contributing, however infinitesimally, almost imperceptibly to the shaping of your soul."[11]

President Boyd K. Packer instructed that our mind is like a stage with the curtain always up except when we sleep. He then suggested that sometime a shady thought may creep in and attract our attention. To clear the stage of our mind from such thoughts, President Packer recommended we choose sacred music including hymns to replace the uninvited and shady thoughts. Then he suggested, "...keep the stage active with learning."[12]

Joseph Smith taught that intense belief—knowledge of the truth—is required to do difficult deeds. "For a man to lay down his all, his character and reputation,...his houses, his lands,...his wife and children, and even his own life...requires more than mere belief or supposition that he is doing the will of God; but actual knowledge, realizing that, when these sufferings are ended, he will enter into eternal rest, and be a partaker of the glory of God.[13]

The Influence of Man's Heart (Desires) on His Other Senses of At-one-ment

President Joseph F. Smith taught the pre-eminent role of our desires. He taught that "everything depends—initially and finally—on our desires. These shape our thought patterns. Our desires thus precede our deeds and lie at the very cores of our souls, tilting us toward or away from God (see D&C 4:3). God can "educate our desires" if we let Him.[14]

The scriptures also teach us of the pre-eminent place of our heart's desires. "According to [our] desires...shall it be done unto [us]" (D&C 11:17). The Lord will work with us even if, at first, we "can no more than desire," but are willing to "give place for a portion of [His] words" (Alma 32:27). A small foothold is all He needs!

Perhaps one reason the scriptures give particular attention to the desires of our hearts is because it is not always possible to perform the deed even if it is wished for with full purpose of heart. For example, in the parable of the laborers, a householder hires workers throughout the day. Those hired last worked less, not for lack of desire, but because they were not offered the opportunity—"no man hath hired us." The implication was that these laborers were willing to work, but lacked opportunity. The parable concludes with the householder paying the laborers all the same wage because they had the same desires, but faced different opportunities to perform their labors (see Matthew 20:1–16).

Clearly, righteous desires lead to righteous beliefs. In effect, our minds will never understand nor believe what our hearts despise. One couplet reports, "A man convinced against his will is of the same opinion still." On the other hand, we are unlikely to desire something which we believe is impossible to obtain. For example, in Aesop's fable, the fox no longer desires the grapes when he comes to believe they are impossible to reach.

President Spencer W. Kimball noted our desire to learn must precede our learning. In a letter to an unbeliever, President Kimball wrote, "I realize I cannot convince you against your will, but I know I can help you if you will only listen and let me call to your attention some salient truths, and if you will listen with a prayer and a desire to know that what I say is true."[15]

Alma described the connection between what man desires and what he does. "And it is requisite with the justice of God that men should be judged according to their works; and if their works were good in this life, [then] the desires of their hearts were good, that they should also, at the last day, be restored unto that which is good" (Alma 41:3). In Proverbs we read that the understanding and desires of a man's heart ultimately determine who he is— "For as [man] thinketh in his heart so is he" (Proverbs 23:7).

One reason for the powerful effect of our desires on what we think, then envision, and then do is because the Spirit is able to enlighten our minds only if we desire it. "And they that will harden their hearts, to them is given the lesser portion of the word until they know nothing concerning his mysteries; and then they are taken captive by the devil, and led by his will down to destruction. Now this is what is meant by the chains of hell" (Alma 12:11).

The Influence of Man's Feet (Deeds) on His Other Senses of At-one-ment

Just as our beliefs and desires influence our visions and deeds, sometimes our deeds can change our beliefs and desires. For instance, when our bodies experience afflictions, our desires and beliefs may change. Amulek describes such a connection. "And as ye have *desired* of my beloved brother that he should make known unto you what ye should do, because of your afflictions; and he hath spoken somewhat unto you to prepare your *minds*" (Alma 34:3; emphasis added).

The scriptures teach that only by doing what the Lord commands can we gain a fulness of understanding of the mind and heart. "And truth is knowledge of things as they are, and as they were, and as they are to come. And no man receiveth a fulness unless he keepeth his commandments. He that keepeth his commandments receiveth truth and light until he is glorified in truth and knoweth all things....And that wicked one cometh and taketh away light and truth, through disobedience, from the children of men, and because of the tradition of their fathers" (D&C 93:24,27–28, 39).

Elder Delbert L. Stapley taught the importance of repeatedly doing—not merely making good resolves—until these good habits become part of our character. "Good habits are not acquired simply by making good resolves, though the thought must precede the action. Good habits are developed in the workshop of our daily lives. It is not in the great moments of test and trial that character is built. That is only when it is displayed. The habits that direct our lives and form our character are fashioned in the often uneventful, commonplace routine of life. They are acquired by practice."[16]

John A. Widtsoe taught that wisdom is the result of wisely applying knowledge. Thus, to gain wisdom we must not only know the truth, but we must live according to the truth we possess. "Thus it often happens that a person of limited knowledge, but who earnestly and prayerfully obeys the law, rises to a higher intelligence or wisdom, than one of vast Gospel learning who does not comply in his daily life with the requirements of the Gospel. Obedience to law is a mark of intelligence."[17]

Abraham Lincoln summarized the connection between deeds and feelings when he said, "When I do good I feel good and when I don't do good I don't feel good."[18]

The Influence of Man's Hands (Vision) on His Other Senses of At-one-ment

Man cannot act without a vision, a spiritual creation. Man's visions often take the form of goals and plans for obtaining the desired outcome created as an image. In the beginning God created all things spiritually before they were created physically. Similarly, our visions are like a spiritual creation for our physical creations to follow (see Moses 3:5). Thus, vision precedes the act and without a vision the people perish (see Proverbs 29:18). Thus, the Lord prepares His prophets by providing them a vision.

The At-one-ment of Man's Senses

The soul of man consisting of his spirit and his body (see D&C 88:15) and enlivened by the Light of Christ (see D&C 84:46) experiences at-one-ment or separation with his mind, heart, hands, and feet. Whether or not man's senses are in harmony or divided depends on whether they are controlled primarily by natural man appetites of the physical body or by the influence of our spirits enlivened by the Holy Ghost. Elder David Bednar taught that the precise nature of the test of mortality can be summarized by the following questions: "Will my body rule over my spirit, or will my spirit rule over my body? Will I yield to the enticing of the natural man or to the eternal man?"[19]

Alma challenged his son Shiblon to seek for spiritual control over the natural man. "See that ye bridle all your passions, that ye may be filled with love; see that ye refrain from idleness" (Alma 38:12). The metaphor is instructive. Just as a bridled horse under the command of its rider can provide powerful service and directed travel, so can our bridled passions under the command and direction of our enlightened spirits direct our bodies to wholesome and helpful pursuits. On the other hand, an unbridled and strong horse, like uncontrolled passions, cannot be at-one with its rider who lacks control over the animal.

When man's beliefs, desires, visions, and deeds are directed by his spirit, he experiences at-one-ment with his best self, others, and God. When the appetites of the natural man and spirit of the eternal man are in conflict, man feels a loss of integrity and experiences separation from others and God. The separation from God that results from yielding to the natural man is described with the powerful metaphor for separation, that of the spiritual death (see Alma 12:16).

The importance of the at-one-ment between our body and spirit is illustrated by another metaphor. Paul compares our bodies to a temple—"Know ye not that your body is the temple of the Holy Ghost which is in you, which ye have of God, and ye are not your own?" (1 Corinthians 6:19).

A temple is a sacred place where God can dwell and in which man can come into His presence and learn of Him. However, if the temple is despoiled by worldly barters and the presence of evil and unprepared persons, then God refuses to dwell there. And, even if man comes to the defiled temple, he will not find God. Similarly, our bodies directed toward pure purposes by the Holy Ghost can provide a sacred place for our righteous spirits to dwell in the light (see Mosiah 2:37).

Conflict and Harmony of Our Senses

It is possible for our feet to act out of concert with our hearts, minds, and hands. When this occurs we act hypocritically or practice priestcraft. In other instances the tug of the natural man on our thoughts, desires, and visions wrest control of these from the influence of the Lord's Spirit and lead us to do disastrous deeds. Indeed, the influence of the natural man can be so powerful over our senses of at-one-ment that their subjugation is described with the metaphor of "being chained."

Yet, our senses of at-one-ment reside together and interdependently in our soul and seek for harmony or at-one-ment with "the natural man or the eternal man." Thus, a lack of harmony between our minds, hearts, hands, and feet produces internal discomfort and is resisted. An insightful scripture teaches that it is impossible to long maintain inconsistency between them because one or the other will eventually win. "No man can serve two masters: for either he will hate the one, and love the other; or else he will hold to the one, and despise the other. Ye cannot serve God and mammon" (Matthew 6:24).

One example of the discomfort produced by a lack of harmony among his senses of at-one-ment was the rich young ruler who came to the Savior desiring to know what was required to gain eternal life. The Savior reviewed for him the laws. The laws he knew and had kept from his youth. But when instructed to sell his riches and give the proceeds to the poor, he went away sorrowing for he loved his possessions more than eternal life (see Matthew 19:16–26).

Mark Twain wrote about the difficulty of attempting to do a deed that is not in harmony with our desires when he has Huckleberry

Finn declare, "I about made up my mind to pray, and see if I couldn't try to quit being the kind of a boy I was and be better. So I kneeled down. But the words wouldn't come. Why wouldn't they? It warn't no use to try and hide it from Him. Nor from ME, neither. I knowed very well why they wouldn't come. It was because my heart warn't right; it was because I warn't square; it was because I was playing double. I was letting ON to give up sin, but away inside of me I was holding on to the biggest one of all. I was trying to make my mouth SAY I would do the right thing and the clean thing..., but deep down in me I knowed it was a lie, and He knowed it. You can't pray a lie—I found that out."[20]

A lack of harmony between our minds and hearts is described in the scriptures as being double minded. James the brother of Jesus taught that a double minded man is unstable in all his ways (see James 1:8). This lack of stability is resolved in favor of evil when one sin leads to another. Bruce R. McConkie wrote that "once Lucifer gets a firm hold over one human weakness, he also applies his power to kindred weaknesses."[21] For example, adultery leads to lying.

In contrast, one righteous act leaves us stronger to resist evil the next time it appears. Shakespeare put these words in the mouth of Hamlet:

Refrain tonight,
And that shall lend a kind of easiness
To the next abstinence: the next more easy;
For use almost can change the stamp of nature,
And either master the devil, or throw him out
With wondrous potency.[22]

The Savior taught that at-one-ment of one's senses is their natural state. "O generation of vipers, how can ye, being evil, speak good things? for out of the abundance of the heart the mouth speaketh. A good man out of the good treasure of the heart bringeth forth good things: and an evil man out of the evil treasure bringeth forth evil things" (Matthew 12:34–35).

Finally, we all struggle for internal at-one-ment between our senses of at-one-ment directed by the Lord's spirit and by the tugs of the natural man. We can take some comfort in knowing that our struggles have plagued the prophets as well. Consider Nephi's struggle.

"I am encompassed about, because of the temptations and the sins which do so easily beset me. . . . And why should I yield to sin, because of my flesh? Yea, why should I give way to temptations, that the evil one have place in my heart to destroy my peace and afflict my soul? Why am I angry because of mine enemy? Awake, my soul! No longer droop in sin. Rejoice, O my heart and give place no more for the enemy of my soul" (2 Nephi 4:18, 27–28).

Yet Nephi won the battle for harmony and achieved the desired at-one-ment of his senses and soul with God. King Benjamin offered the key. "For the natural man is an enemy to God, and has been from the fall of Adam, and will be, forever and ever, unless he yields to the enticings of the Holy Spirit, and putteth off the natural man and becometh a saint through the atonement of Christ the Lord, and becometh as a child, submissive, meek, humble, patient, full of love, willing to submit to all things which the Lord seeth fit to inflict upon him, even as a child doth submit to his father" (Mosiah 3:19).

We too can win the battle for harmony waged between the natural man and the spiritual man. We win the battle for harmony with God every time we yield to the influence of the Holy Ghost and separate ourselves from the natural man by becoming submissive, meek, humble, patient, and yielding to the impressions of the Holy Ghost—like a child who trusts her parents.

℘ ℘

Amy and John returned home and found Frank shooting hoops in the driveway. Mark was reading a book he had brought home from school. Sam, much to Amy and John's dismay, had called one of her friends on the phone and was chatting away about—nothing really. Finally, Heidi was creating a little community consisting of her dolls who had much to say to each other. John took charge. "All right...everyone in for prayers." And they all came in because even though they were different they each in their own way enjoyed the feeling of being one and belonging to a family.

Conclusions

We all have had the experience on a hot day of filling a glass with ice and water and noting how the temperature of the water and ice become one. Similarly, we have noted on a cold day how hot chocolate and marshmallows also soon harmonize to the same temperature. The physical law of harmony applied to things spiritual makes urgent our yielding control of our senses to the influence of the Lord. Our minds, hearts, hands, and feet, like ice and water and hot chocolate and marshmallows, seek for harmony. They influence each other. Yet, if we had to choose, we would say man's desires matter most.

NOTES

1. *Gospel Principles,* (1997), 13.

2. Dallin H. Oaks, "Teaching and Learning by the Spirit," *Ensign*, March 1997, 13.

3. Harold B. Lee, *Stand Ye in Holy Places,* (1974), 92; quoted by Dallin H. Oaks in *Pure in Heart*, (1988), viii.

4. Boyd K. Packer, "Revelation in a Changing World," *Ensign,* November 1989, 14.

5. William Wilson, *Old Testament Word Studies* (1978), 205; quoted by W. Craig Zwick in "The Lord Thy God Will Hold Thy Hand," *Ensign*, November 2003, 34.

6. Quoted by Thomas L. Friedman, *Longitudes and Attitudes: Exploring the World after September 11*, (2003), 444.

7. Bible Dictionary, 648.

8. Daniel K. Judd, "The Spirit of Christ: A Light amid Darkness," *Liahona*, May 2001, 18.

9. *Doctrines of Salvation,* compiled by Bruce R. McConkie, (1954–56), 1:147.

10. Kenneth L. Higbee, *BYU Speeches of the Year,* (1964), 8.

11. David O. McKay, *Man May Know for Himself: Teachings of President David O. McKay,* compiled by Clare Middlemiss, (1967), 173.

12. Boyd K. Packer, *Teach Ye Diligently,* (1975), 46–47.

13. Joseph Smith, *Lectures on Faith,* (reprinted 1985), 65, 68.

14. Joseph F. Smith, *Gospel Doctrine,* 5th ed., (1939), 297.

15. Spencer W. Kimball, "Absolute Truth," *Ensign*, September 1978, 3.

16. Delbert L. Stapley, "Good Habits Develop Good Character," *Ensign,* November 1974, 20.

17. John A. Widtsoe, Conference Report, April 1938, 50.

18. Marion D. Hanks, Conference Report, October 1967, 59.

19. David A. Bednar, "Ye Are the Temple of God," *Ensign,* September 2001, 14.

20. Mark Twain, *Adventures of Huckleberry Finn*, (1899), 192.

21. Bruce R. McConkie, *Doctrinal New Testament Commentary,* vol.1, 277.

22. William Shakespeare, *Hamlet*, act 3, scene 4.

Chapter Six

REPENTANCE AND RESTORING AT-ONE-MENT

*Now I would that ye should remember that God has
said that the inward vessel shall be cleansed first,
and then shall the outer vessel be cleansed also.*

—Alma 60:23

CR ED

Frank was seated in front of the TV watching "Dancing with the Stars." Some of the female dancers were sensually dressed and their gyrating and jerking movements stimulated his senses. Frank was transfixed and visually irritated when his Mom commanded, "Turn that off!" "Why?" Frank responded resentfully. Amy patiently explained, "Because the women are half dressed and watching them drives away the Spirit." "You are so out of touch, Mom. There's nothing wrong with this program. They're just dancing!" Frank replied defensively as he stormed out of the room, pushing Heidi aside and scattering her make believe tea party set on the way out of the house. Amy despaired. "Frank seems so angry and unconnected to the family as of late," she said to no one in particular.

When John returned home from work, Amy recalled the unhappy exchange between her and Frank. John found Frank in the driveway shooting hoops. Frank greeted his dad cheerfully almost as though nothing had happened. "Frank, what's going on?" John queried. "What do you mean?" Frank responded evasively. John put his arm on Frank's shoulder and invited, "Let's go for a walk."

The Sorrowful Steps of Separation and Sin

Sin and Separations

Frank—like all of us do when we sin—experienced the sorrowful steps of separation. Essential for our joy and progress is the plan for restoring our at-one-ment with our best self, others, and God. The sorrowful steps of separation have a too familiar pattern that we must learn about and avoid.

God's commandments direct us to at-one-ment and joy. When one knows God's commandments and chooses to disobey them, "to him it is sin" (James 4:17). Sin is easily sold because it focuses one's attention on oneself and promises that our senses will be saturated with stimulation. However, sin with its focus on selfishness, collides with our integrity that demands we do what we know is right.

Then, when we yield to temptation and lose our integrity, we more naturally commit sins that separate us from others. Elder Neal A. Maxwell explained: "By focusing on oneself, it is naturally easier to bear false witness if it serves one's purpose. It is easier to ignore one's parents instead of honoring them. It is easier to steal, because what one wants prevails. It is easier to covet, since the selfish conclude that nothing should be denied them . . . . The selfish individual thus seeks to please not God, but himself. He will even break a covenant in order to fix an appetite. Selfishness has little time to regard the sufferings of others seriously, hence the love of many waxes cold."[1]

Indeed, bearing false witness, ignoring one's parents, stealing from others, and coveting the possessions of others are all mile markers on the road to alone-ment. As we lose our integrity and separate ourselves from others through sin, we automatically separate ourselves from God because we rebel against Him. We may not recognize our separation from God because sin deadens our senses—which were once enlivened by God's Spirit which we no longer long for. Thus, the desire to sin is significantly connected to the desire for alone-ment from God and others and at-one-ment with the things of the world.

The Separating Sequence of Sin

Helaman succinctly summarizes the sequence from at-one-ment to separation and sin. In the initial stage of the separation sequence, the people shifted their focus from God and the well-being of others to riches and things. "They began to set their hearts upon their riches." Then they used their riches to separate themselves from each other "that they might be lifted up one above another." Finally, separated and insensitive to each other's well being, they could more easily commit serious sins that not only affected property but inflicted harm on others, and "they began to commit secret murders, and to rob and to plunder, that they might get gain" (Helaman 6:17).

Sin and Our Desensitized Senses of At-One-Ment

As we shift our focus from God and serving one another to a focus on things, we separate ourselves from others and deaden our senses of at-one-ment. Our senses of at-one-ment depend upon our receiving revelations through the Light of Christ and the Holy Ghost to our minds and to our hearts, where the Holy Ghost dwells (see D&C 8:2). When we treat lightly the things of God, we receive no such revelations.

The Lord revealed to Joseph Smith, "Your minds in times past have been darkened because of unbelief, and because you have treated lightly the things you have received" (D&C 84:54). Nephi, the disciple who prepared the people for Christ's coming, described the deadened senses of at-one-ment among the people of his time. "[He] being eye-witness to their quick return from righteousness unto their wickedness and abominations; therefore, being grieved for the hardness of their hearts and the blindness of their minds—went forth among them in that same year, and began to testify, boldly, repentance and remission of sins through faith on the Lord Jesus Christ" (3 Nephi 7:15–16).

In the days of Mormon and his son Moroni, the people's senses of at-one-ment became completely deadened and their separation so complete that they could commit all classes of depravity. Mormon described their condition. "And they [the "Nephites"] have become strong in their perversion; and they are alike brutal, sparing none, neither old nor young; and they delight in everything save that which is good; and the suffering of our women and our children upon all the face of this land doth exceed everything; yea, tongue cannot tell, neither can it be written.... Behold, thou knowest the wickedness of this people; thou knowest that they are without principle, and past feeling; and their wickedness doth exceed that of the Lamanites" (Moroni 9:19–20).

Repentance and Restoring At-one-ment

There is only one remedy for sin-caused sorrow and separateness. The remedy is repentance. "For behold, I say unto you that as many...as will repent are the covenant people of the Lord;...for the Lord covenanteth with none save it be with them that repent and believe in his Son, who is the Holy One of Israel" (2 Nephi 30:2).

The definition of repentance means "a turning of the heart and will to God," "a fresh view about God, about oneself, and about the world," or a "renunciation of sin to which we are naturally inclined."[2] Alma added that repentance includes coming to the knowledge of God, and to rejoice in Jesus Christ our Redeemer (see Alma 37:9).

If we are repenting and turning toward God we must be turning away from the things that oppose God. Repentance is not optional for those who desire at-one-ment and eternal life with God.

There are two phases of repentance. Moroni compared the first phase to cleansing the inner vessel and second phase to cleansing the outer vessel. The first phase of repentance, cleansing the inner vessel, restores our integrity. The second phase of repentance, cleansing the outer vessel, restores our at-one-ment with others.

Once we have cleansed both—the inner vessel and regained our integrity and the outer vessel and restored our at-one-ment with others—we will have automatically regained our at-one-ment with God. Consider next the two phases of repentance designed to restore our integrity and our at-one-ment with others and God.

Repentance—Cleansing the Inner Vessel

The Inner Vessel and Integrity

The repentance process that restores at-one-ment must begin with our efforts to regain our integrity, cleansing the inner vessel. "And why beholdest thou the mote that is in thy brother's eye, but considerest not the beam that is in thine own eye? Or how wilt thou say to thy brother, Let me pull out the mote out of thine eye; and, behold, a beam is in thine own eye? Thou hypocrite, first cast out the beam out of thine own eye; and then shalt thou see clearly to cast out the mote out of thy brother's eye" (Matthew 7:3–5). Similarly, Chief Capitan Moroni admonished, "Now I would that ye should remember that God has said that the inward vessel shall be cleansed first, and then shall the outer vessel be cleansed also" (Alma 60:23).

We surely cannot expect to declare the word of God unless we have first obtained it (see D&C 11:21). We cannot expect God to forgive us unless we have forgiven others of their offenses toward us. We cannot help others develop their testimony of the Savior unless we have gained one ourselves.

President Benson taught a similar lesson. "The Lord works from the inside out. The world [works] from the outside in. The world would take people out of the slums. Christ takes the slums out of people, and then they take themselves out of the slums. The world would mould men by changing their environment. Christ changes men, who then change their environment. The world would shape human behavior, but Christ can change human nature."[3]

The gospel message is that to restore the at-one-ment lost through sin, we must first regain our integrity. After our integrity has been regained, then we must seek to restore Zion by rebuilding at-one-ment with others. Then, and only then, can we qualify for at-one-ment with God and salvation.

The Repentance Process and Our Sense of At-one-ment

The repentance process that restores our integrity engages all of our senses of at-one-ment. "But if the children shall repent, or the children's children, and turn to the Lord their God, with all their hearts and with all their might, mind, and strength, and restore four–fold for all their trespasses wherewith they have trespassed, or wherewith their fathers have trespassed, or their fathers' fathers, then thine indignation shall be turned away" (D&C 98:47).

The first step of repentance engages our minds as we learn what God requires, we recognize that we are distant from His standard, and we confess our differences. The Lord revealed this step to Joseph Smith. "By this ye may know if a man repenteth of his sins—behold, he will confess them and forsake them" (D&C 58:43). This confession, as needed, is extended to all the objects of our at-one-ment—to ourselves, to church leaders, and to God.

In the second step we engage our hearts in the repentance process. In our hearts we feel remorse for our separating sins and desire to return to His ways. "And behold, I have given you the law and the commandments of my Father, that ye shall believe in me, and that ye shall repent of your sins, and come unto me with a broken heart and a contrite spirit" (3 Nephi 12:19).

In the third step, we create spiritually our path to at-one-ment. We envision a path that repairs the separations we caused by our sins. We create spiritually "a fresh view about God, about ourselves, and about the world." Then we come to more fully rejoice in Christ.

Finally, our repentance requires that we accept our responsibility for our sins and that we act—to repair past wrongs and do right things in the future. President Harold B. Lee described our sense of doing represented by our feet. "Following confession, one in sin must show forth the fruits of his repentance by good deeds that are weighted against the bad. He must make proper restitution to the limit of his power to restore that which he has taken away or to repair the damage he has done."[4]

The repentance process that awakens our senses of understanding, feeling, visioning, and doing was described by Alma the Younger who needed to repent because of his earlier efforts to destroy the Church. Alma described his repentance that followed the visit of an angel.

First in his *mind* he recognized his sins and iniquities. "[I] saw that I had rebelled against my God, and that I had not kept his holy commandments" (Alma 36:13). Then in his *heart* Alma felt Godly sorrow for his sins for which he was tormented with indescribable horror (see Alma 36:14). Then while in a state of anguish, his *vision* changed. He remembered the teachings of his father about the Lord Jesus Christ, and how Christ would come to atone for the sins of the world (see Alma 36:17).

As he caught hold of this thought he prayed to our Lord and Savior, and he "could remember [his] pains no more; yea, [he] was harrowed up by the memory of [his] sins no more" (Alma 36:19). Then from that time forward, Alma put his *feet* on the path of good works and attempted to undo the wrongs he had committed (see Alma 36:24).

Finally, the sons of Mosiah provided another example of the repentance process. After they recognized their sins, they were stung by remorse and "they traveled throughout all the land of Zarahemla, and among all the people who were under the reign of king Mosiah, zealously striving to repair all the injuries which they had done to the church, confessing all their sins, and publishing all the things which they had seen, and explaining the prophecies and the scriptures to all who desired to hear them" (Mosiah 27:34–35).

Repentance—Cleansing the Outer Vessel

After we have sinned, repented, and had our integrity restored, then we are commanded to cleanse the outer vessel. This process clearly focuses on creating and maintaining the sense of at-one-ment between us and others. The road that, when taken, restores our at-one-ment with others requires that we do for them what we ask Christ to do for us. The process is described next.

Forgive Others

When we sin, we create debts we cannot repay. As a result, it is only with the help of the Savior's Atonement that the price of sin is paid. But in the process of relying on the Savior's grace to pay the debt that rescues us from Satan's awful grasp, separations, and sorrows, we incur a new debt—a debt to the Savior. The discharge of this debt requires that we follow the example of the Savior. "Verily, verily, I say unto you, this is my gospel; and ye know the things that ye must do in my church; for the works which ye have seen me do that shall ye also do; for that which ye have seen me do even that shall ye do" (3 Nephi 27:21).

During His ministry the Savior performed many great works. But the greatest and the most to be recognized and praised was His forgiving us our sins on condition of repentance. His Atonement gave Him this grace, to pay the debt for sins we have committed, a debt that He did not owe. So, the "things we must do," "the work that we have seen Him do," is to forgive sins. But what sins can we forgive? Surely, we cannot forgive all sins or all debts. Indeed the only debts that we can forgive are those that others owe us. These we have not only the capacity, but the obligation to forgive.

Indeed, our own forgiveness requires that we forgive others their trespasses. This act of at-one-ment with others is what the Lord requires of us to obtain our at-one-ment with God. The Lord taught in both the Old and New World that "if ye forgive not men their trespasses neither will your Father forgive your trespasses" (see 3 Nephi 13:15; Matthew 6:15; Mark 11:26).

One reason forgiving others of an offense is essential to regaining our integrity and restoring our at-one-ment with others is that failure to forgive predisposes us to commit the same or a similar sin. Indeed the weakness we are least likely to forgive in others is one we possess ourselves. Many who abuse their wives, husbands, colleagues, and children were themselves abused and have not been able to forgive the offender.

Many who have had trespasses committed against them and are unwilling to forgive are locked in a quest for reprisal. It is this quest that propels them to sin. The reprisal, however, is often an exaggerated form of the original offense and is often committed against the innocent. The Hatfields and McCoys feuded over the loss of a pig. Their unwillingness to forgive caused the loss of innocent human life. In addition, failure to forgive often leads to the involvement of others in committing the same or a similar sin.

I have painfully watched entire wards and families alienated by an acrimonious divorce. Who do you think will be held accountable for the separation of so many? He who wouldn't forgive will be held accountable for the greater sin (see D&C 64:9).

Another reason why cleansing the outer vessel requires that we forgive others is because those forgiven are more likely to forgive us and others in return. This application of the principle of restoration, "for that which ye do send out shall return unto you again and be restored," leads us to at-one-ment with others.

The connection between forgiving and repenting can be explained another way. The faults we look for in others are often so easily recognized because they are the ones we possess. For instance, Laman and Lemuel were unwilling to forgive Nephi of an imagined sin of seeking to rule over them because, in fact, it was the sin they were most anxious to commit. Failing to forgive others is merely evidence that we have not repented of the sin ourselves.

Another reason our repentance requires that we forgive others is because failure to do so separates us from God. If we fail to forgive, we in effect assert that God is unable or unwilling to apply the required number of stripes. Our lack of confidence in God's justice requires that we supervise His work. So in effect, when we are unwilling to forgive, we deny God's omniscience and goodness and become gods unto ourselves. Thus, by our unwillingness to forgive, we deny our faith, and lacking faith, we fail in our application of the first principle of the gospel.

Finally, there is one more reason why we must cleanse the outer vessel by forgiving others. It is because those who refuse to do so frequently engage in recruiting others to support them in their separateness. For example, Laman and Lemuel enlisted others to assist them in their efforts to take Nephi's life (see 2 Nephi 5:3). When Amlici acted against the established laws of the land and had himself appointed king, his first act was to command his followers to take up arms against their brothers (see Alma 2:10). Finally, when the king-men had convinced themselves that their genealogy bestowed upon them special privileges, they cheered on their enemies—the Lamanites who were seeking the destruction of the Nephites (see Alma 51:13). This pattern is so often repeated—those in sin petitioning others to hear their claims against the just.

Judge Not

We will never need to forgive others if we first refuse to judge them guilty of a crime. So the Lord commanded that we refrain from judgments that lead to separations. "Judge not, and ye shall not be judged: condemn not, and ye shall not be condemned: forgive, and ye shall be forgiven" (Luke 6:37). And in the case of an actual offense and the offended appeals for forgiveness and reconciliation, the Lord counseled, "If thy brother trespass against thee, rebuke him; and if he repent, forgive him. And if he trespass against thee seven times in a day, and seven times in a day turn again to thee, saying, I repent; thou shalt forgive him" (Luke 17:3–4).

In contrast to pride-prompted judgments that separate us are righteous judgments. These righteous judgments highlight our separations and differences and prescribe the path to reconciliation. The responsibilities for making righteous judgments are vested in those with welfare promoting responsibilities—parents for children, bishops for ward members, stake presidents for stake members, and everyone else who has a sphere of responsibility assigned him. To all of these shepherds, the Lord commands, "judge righteous judgments" (Mosiah 29:43).

Be Equal

In addition to forgiving the trespass of others, there are other acts of at-one-ment that in effect cleanse the outer vessel. One such act is to eliminate the material differences between us. The Lord commanded, "Nevertheless, in your temporal things you shall be equal, and this not grudgingly, otherwise the abundance of the manifestations of the Spirit shall be withheld" (D&C 70:14). Then elsewhere the Lord explained, "For if ye are not *equal* in earthly things ye cannot be *equal* in obtaining heavenly things; for if you will that I give unto you a place in the celestial world, you must prepare yourselves by doing the things which I have commanded you and required of you" (D&C 78:6–7; emphasis added).

To connect our material equality to at-one-ment and remission of sins, the Lord taught through His prophet-king Benjamin, "And now, for the sake of these things which I have spoken unto you—that is, for the sake of *retaining a remission of your sins* from day to day, that ye may walk guiltless before God—I would that ye should impart of your substance to the poor, every man according to that which he hath, such as feeding the hungry, clothing the naked, visiting the sick and administering to their relief, both spiritually and temporally, according to their wants" (Mosiah 4:26; emphasis added).

Refuse To Take Offense

Another cleansing the outer vessel requirement was included in the Lord's sermon at the temple and on the mount. He taught that we should refuse to take separating offense at what others do. "Ye have heard that it hath been said by them of old time, and it is also written before you, that thou shalt not kill, and whosoever shall kill shall be in danger of the judgment of God; But I say unto you, that whosoever is angry with his brother shall be in danger of his judgment" (3 Nephi 12:21–22).

Not only should we not take offense, we should not give offense, since both actions divide. And if we have given offense, we must seek to be reconciled. The Lord taught, "Therefore, if ye shall come unto me, or shall desire to come unto me, and rememberest that thy brother hath aught against thee—Go thy way unto thy brother, and first be reconciled to thy brother, and then come unto me with full purpose of heart, and I will receive you" (3 Nephi 12:23–24). However, to reconcile an offended brother is not always easy. As we learn in Proverbs, "A brother offended is harder to be won than a strong city: and their contentions are like the bars of a castle" (Proverbs 18:19). Perhaps the analogy of those offended being held captive behind castle bars explains why the lists of inactive members are so long and require such deliberate and delicate labor to be reclaimed.

One way we can avoid giving offense is by refusing to be disagreeable and by agreeing with "thine adversary quickly while thou are in the way with him" (3 Nephi 12:25). A wound not cleansed provides opportunities for germs to work their wickedness against the body. A disagreement unresolved rather than being quickly mended, deepens the separation among former friends.

Finally, to complete His instruction on cleansing the outer vessel, Jesus declared, "And blessed is he, whosoever shall not be offended in me" (Matthew 11:6). The Savior provided the perfect example of how to avoid taking offense. "For even hereunto were ye called: because Christ also suffered for us, leaving us an example, that ye should follow his steps: who did no sin, neither was guile found in his mouth: who, when he was reviled, reviled not again; when he suffered, he threatened not" (1 Peter 2:21–23).

Paul gave more instructions on how to maintain our at-one-ment. When we find those who seek divisions we should avoid them. "Now I beseech you, brethren, mark them which cause divisions and offenses contrary to the doctrine which ye have learned; and avoid them" (Romans 16:17). And the Lord revealed to Joseph Smith that those responsible for divisive deeds should be confronted. "And if thy brother or sister offend thee, thou shalt take him or her between him or her and thee alone; and if he or she confess thou shalt be reconciled" (D&C 42:88).

Under God's direction, Enoch preached repentance. As the people repented, they became of one heart, one mind, and dwelt in righteousness and there were no poor among them. And then they were taken into heaven to be eternally one with God (see Moses 7:21).

The Evidence of Repentance

We begin the repentance process by regaining our integrity. The process depends on and cannot be completed without Christ's Atonement. After regaining our integrity, including clean hands and a pure heart, repentance requires that we restore our at-one-ment with others. And the evidence of having completed both steps is our desire for the well-being of and at-one-ment with others, first with friends and family and then with even our enemies.

Enos, for example, first gained integrity by repenting of his sins and being forgiven, and then sought for Zion and the welfare of his friends, and last of all his enemies. "Enos, thy sins are forgiven thee, and thou shalt be blessed. And I, Enos, knew that God could not lie; wherefore, my guilt was swept away" (Enos 1:5–6). "Now, it came to pass that when I had heard these words I began to feel a desire for the welfare of my brethren, the Nephites; wherefore, I did pour out my whole soul unto God for them" (Enos 1:9). Then last of all Enos prayed, "My faith began to be unshaken in the Lord; and I prayed unto him with many long strugglings for my brethren, the Lamanites" (Enos 1:11).

Ammon and the other sons of Mosiah first waded through the depths of suffering to repent and regain their integrity and only then internalized the well-being of the Lamanites that led them to their missions. "Now they were desirous that salvation should be declared to every creature, for they could not bear that any human soul should perish; yea, even the very thoughts that any soul should endure endless torment did cause them to quake and tremble. And thus did the Spirit of the Lord work upon them, for they were the very vilest of sinners. And the Lord saw fit in his infinite mercy to spare them; nevertheless they suffered much anguish of soul because of their iniquities, suffering much and fearing that they should be cast off forever" (Mosiah 28:3–4).

Father Lehi, who had integrity, could not enjoy the fruit of the tree of life without immediately looking to bless his family with the same fruit. "And it came to pass that I beheld a tree, whose fruit was desirable to make one happy. And it came to pass that I did go forth and partake of the fruit thereof; and I beheld that it was most sweet, above all that I ever before tasted. Yea, and I beheld that the fruit thereof was white, to exceed all the whiteness that I had ever seen. And as I partook of the fruit thereof it filled my soul with exceedingly great joy; wherefore, I began to be desirous that my family should partake of it also; for I knew that it was desirable above all other fruit" (1 Nephi 8:10–12).

The ultimate evidence of forgiveness is salvation and at-one-ment with God. To those who were one and served each other, the Lord declared their at-one-ment with Him. "Come, ye blessed of my Father, inherit the kingdom prepared for you from the foundation of the world" (Matthew 25:34). However, those who were welcomed to at-one-ment with God because of their service to others were surprised and asked, "Lord, when saw we thee an hungered, and fed thee? or thirsty, and gave thee drink? When saw we thee a stranger, and took thee in? or naked, and clothed thee? Or when saw we thee sick, or in prison, and came unto thee?" And the Lord answered, "Verily I say unto you, Inasmuch as ye have done it unto one of the least of these my brethren, ye have done it unto me" (Matthew 25:37–40).

℘ ℘

Frank sat pensively on his bed and wondered about what his dad had tried to teach him during their walk—about sin and separating oneself from others. "I'm not doing anything that separates me from the family," he said out loud to no one in particular. Then he remembered how he had become increasingly annoyed with his younger brother Mark—who wanted to tag along wherever he went. He was especially annoyed when Mark wanted to go to a movie with him and his friends that he knew his parents wouldn't approve. And, he recalled how rude he had been to Sam and her friend when he found them, univited, in his room where he had some questionable posters on the wall.

Just then, Heidi opened his door and somewhat hestitantly

asked, "Do you want to play a game with me?" And she was somewhat surprised when Frank responded enthusiastically, "Of course!"

Conclusion

The ultimate goal of the gospel is eternal life—at-one-ment with God. The path to this at-one-ment is repentance and service. When we strive for integrity through repentance, and Zion through service, we too may be invited to receive salvation and at-one-ment with God and hear the words: "Come, ye blessed of my Father, inherit the kingdom prepared for you from the foundation of the world" (Matthew 25:34).

NOTES

1. Neal A. Maxwell, "Put Off the Natural Man, and Come Off Conqueror," *Ensign*, November 1990, 14.
2. Bible Dictionary, 760.
3. Ezra Taft Benson, Conference Report, October 1985, 4–6.
4. *Teachings of Presidents of the Church: Harold B. Lee*, (2000), 30.

Chapter Seven

OUR NEED FOR AT-ONE-MENT

Every new member [and all the rest of us] needs
three things: a friend, a responsibility, and
nurturing with 'the good word of God.'[1]

—Gordon B. Hinckley

ﾍ ﾌ

A my was busy folding clothes and noticed the dirty dishes piled up from breakfast. Heidi was calling for help from her bedroom, and of course, the phone rang. It was Sister Clark asking for her visiting teaching report. Amy thought to herself, *The problem with a woman's work is not that it's never done, it's that no one ever notices.* She assumed that her family noticed, but wondered if they really knew how much was required to maintain their home. Sometimes her endless cycle of never done duties left her feeling like "Molly Maid"—the difference between them being that she wasn't ever able to leave her work and go home. Yet, she loved an orderly house and was willing to stay up late, if necessary, just to wake up to pleasant surroundings.

She was grateful for her neighbor Andrea who always seemed to come by at the right time. Amy remembered yesterday's visit. They talked, cheered each other up, shared parenting tips, and even philosophized. They reviewed the previous week's Sunday School lesson, expressed their views on the qualifications of the current field of presidential candidates, the war in Iraq, and their flower gardens—and the need for more exercise. Then some of the children started fighting and crying, and Andrea too soon had to leave. But Amy felt refreshed.

Our Four Needs

Associated with each of man's four senses of at-one-ment described in chapter five is a need. Besides our physical need for "bread," we need to see beauty in our surroundings, to feel the love of a friend, to matter to the success of important outcomes, and to know the meaning of important truths. Steven R. Covey and Roger and Rebecca Merrill described these needs as the need to love, to learn, to live (to see beauty), and to leave a legacy (to matter).[2]

The intended purpose of God's creations and man's existence is joy. Standing between man and joy are the fulfillment of his four basic needs. These four needs create within man a spiritual hunger that drives his pursuits and determines what deeds fill his days. Indeed, many of the differences among men and women are simply their understandings of how to best satisfy their fundamental needs. Consider in detail our four needs and how best to satisfy them.

Our Need for Beauty

Associated with man's visual senses of at-one-ment represented by his hands is the need for *beauty*. Beauty is the harmonious combination of created things, an at-one-ment of lights, colors, shapes, sequences, sounds, and ideas that delight the senses and please the mind.[3] Beauty is evidence of God's hand in the creation of the world. So, when we observe and contribute to beauty, we connect ourselves to God and His creations. In the absence of beauty and its close relative, order, man experiences a dreary separateness. Therefore, we need beauty to experience all of the dimensions of at-one-ment.

God recognized man's need for beauty and so, from material without form—void and dark (see Genesis 1:2)—God created (organized) in its place, light (see Genesis 1:3), order, and things which He declared to be very good (see Genesis1:31) and "pleasant to the sight" (Genesis 2:9). Speaking to the Prophet Joseph Smith, God declared the purpose of His Creation. "Yea, all things which come of the earth, in the season thereof, are made for the benefit and the use of man, both to please the eye and to gladden the heart; Yea, for food and for raiment, for taste and for smell, to strengthen the body and to enliven the soul" (D&C 59:18–19).

President Gordon B. Hinckley declared, "I believe in beauty." Continuing, he taught, "I believe in the beauty of nature—the flowers, the fruit, the sky, the peaks, and the plains from which they rise. I see and believe in the beauty of animals. I see and admire beauty in people…I am not concerned whether the skin be fair or dark. I have seen beautiful people in all of the scores of nations through which I have walked. Little children are beautiful everywhere. And so are the aged, whose wrinkled hands and faces speak of struggle and survival."[4]

Edwin Markham described man's basic needs and included among these man's need for beauty. "Three things must a man possess if his soul would live and know life's perfect good—Three things would the all-supplying Father give—bread, beauty and brotherhood."[5]

One of our favorite hymns, a prayer, acknowledges our debt to God for the beauty of His creations which satisfies within us one of our most basic needs. "For the beauty of the earth, for the beauty of the skies…for the beauty of each hour of the day and of the night…Lord of all, to thee we raise this our hymn of grateful praise."[6] "God hath made everything beautiful in his time: also he hath set the world in their heart, so that no man can find out the work that God maketh from the beginning to the end" (Ecclesiastes 3:11).

Satisfying Our Need for Beauty

To satisfy our need for at-one-ment with God's creations, we must extend effort in two directions. First, we must become aware of beauty, the evidence of God's participation in the Creation. Second, we must strive to create beauty where it does not exist.

Elder Richard G. Scott challenged:

> Do you take time to discover each day how beautiful your life can be? How long has it been since you watched the sun set? The departing rays kissing the clouds, trees, hills, and lowlands good night, sometimes tranquilly, sometimes with exuberant bursts of color and form. What of the wonder of a cloudless night when the Lord unveils the marvels of His heavens—the twinkling stars, the moonlight rays—to ignite our imagination with His greatness and glory? How captivating to watch a seed planted in fertile soil germinate, gather strength, and send forth a tiny, seemingly insignificant sprout. Patiently it begins to grow and develop its own character led by the genetic code the Lord has provided to guide its development. With care it surely will become what it is destined to be: a lily, crowned with grace and beauty; a fragrant spearmint plant; a peach; an avocado; or a beautiful blossom with unique delicacy, hue, and fragrance. When last did you observe a tiny rosebud form? Each day it develops new and impressive character, more promise of beauty until it becomes a majestic rose. You are one of the noblest of God's creations. His intent is that your life be gloriously beautiful regardless of your circumstances.[7]

We can become creators of beauty and find joy in the process. We create beauty, at-one-ment, and order among created things when we do such simple things as straighten our rooms, comb our hair, shine our shoes, iron our shirts and blouses, and plant a flower. We create beauty when we order our desks, when we put things back in their proper places, when we prepare a well organized talk, when we mow the lawn, or when we sing an uplifting song.

Our Need to Feel the Love of Friends

Associated with man's emotional senses represented by his heart, is man's need to feel love that establishes an at-one-ment between himself and others and God. Love is the evidence of at-one-ment between God and man. Love is the attribute that most characterizes God and the one that most describes the people of Zion. To love God and others is the most important of all commandments. To feel love, we need friends. Indeed, God has declared Himself to be a friend to man. A friend is one who "loveth at all times" (Proverbs 17:17). God is our friend because He laid down His life for us. We are God's friend when we keep His commandments (see John 15:14).

The Lord often administers to our needs through our friends. During a critical time when young Joseph Smith most needed a friend, the Lord sent Martin Harris. The Prophet Joseph wrote: "The persecution, however, became so intolerable that I was under the necessity of leaving Manchester, and going with my wife to Susquehanna County, in the State of Pennsylvania. While preparing to start—being very poor, and the persecution so heavy upon us that there was no probability that we would ever be otherwise—in the midst of our afflictions we found a friend in a gentleman by the name of Martin Harris, who came to us and gave me fifty dollars to assist us on our journey."[8]

A true friend tells you what you need to hear for your happiness and well-being. A false friend flatters you with what you want to hear. A true friend stays with you even when the wild animals threaten. A false friend flees in the face of danger or the possibility of a new friend with more status. A true friend is happy when you're happy and mourns with you when you mourn.

There is no more fundamental need than to be loved—even among animals. In a remarkable experiment, conducted by Harry Harlow in a University of Wisconsin laboratory, he found that monkeys need love. In an effort to prevent the spread of a disease among monkeys imported from India to the healthy monkeys in his lab, Harlow and his staff attempted to solve the disease problem by isolating the sick monkeys from healthy ones, including healthy newborn monkeys from diseased mothers. The isolation dumbfounded the newborn monkeys and often they would sit rocking, staring into the air, and sucking their thumbs. Later when the isolated monkeys matured and were brought together to breed, they backed away from each other and refused contact.

Then researchers found that the little monkeys were fanatically attached to cloth diapers that lined the cages to provide a little softness and warmth against the floor. Then Harlow demonstrated that the cloth was substituting for a mother's love. His idea that mother's love was essential for a healthy monkey was in opposition to the prevailing theory—that babies didn't love their mothers or need them, and that the only relationship was based on being fed. Harlow's concluding observation was that "food is sustenance, but a good hug is life itself."[9]

Speaking of the need for love by the young [and old], Clark Swain wrote, "Babies and children need love just as they need vitamin C and whole grain cereal. It is impossible to give a baby too much love. One who receives insufficient love may become retarded in his physical growth and his personality development. He may become emotionally and physically ill."[10]

The English word *friend* is related to the Old English word *fréond* which is the present participle of the verb *fréon,* meaning to love. So friends are persons who love each other. The connection between friend and love is also found in Spanish where the word for friend is *amigo* and the word meaning to love is *amar.* In Latin a similar relationship exists between the words for friend and to love, *amicus* and *amare.*[11]

Friends desire each other's well-being and contribute to each other being better. Elder Marvin J. Ashton one time reminisced that a friend has been defined as a person who is willing to take me the way I am. He then went on to add that we are something less than a real friend if we leave a person the same way we find him. "Acts of a friend should result in self-improvement, better attitudes, self-reliance, comfort, consolation, self-respect, and better welfare. Certainly the word *friend* is misused if it is identified with a person who contributes to our delinquency, misery, and heartaches."[12]

More recently, the First Presidency has counseled, "Everyone needs good friends. Your circle of friends will greatly influence your thinking and behavior, just as you will theirs. When you share common values with your friends, you can strengthen and encourage each other. If some of your friends are shy and do not feel included, be particularly sensitive to their feelings and go out of your way to pull them into the influence of your strong circle of good friends. Together you can maintain a high standard of gospel living."[13]

Joseph Smith, a great friend to many, declared, "Friendship is one of the grand fundamental principles of 'Mormonism'; [it is designed] to revolutionize and civilize the world, and cause wars and contentions to cease and men to become friends and brothers."[14] One of our favorite hymns emphasizes the importance of friends.

> What greater gift dost thou bestow,
> What greater goodness can we know
> Than Christlike friends, whose gentle ways
> Strengthen our faith, enrich our days.[15]

Finally, we ask, how do we satisfy our need for love? We cannot feel love without offering service and we often best feel the love of others in their kind acts of assistance. Perfect love, the Savior taught, is making a perfect sacrifice for those we love. "Greater love hath no man than this, that a man lay down his life for his friends" (John 15:13). Moreover, love not only lays down her life for her friends, but she lives for them as well. When they are sick, she visits them. When they are in need, she shares what she has. When they are filled with sorrow, she comforts them. And when they have joy, she rejoices.

Our Need to Matter

Associated with man's sense of doing (represented by his feet) is man's need to matter. This need is satisfied by his at-one-ment with the work of building mankind, by working at a "meaningful" assignment. The most meaningful assignments are found in the Lord's kingdom and involve the assignment of bringing souls to Christ.

President Spencer W. Kimball once described the benefits of providing service. "When we are engaged in the service of our fellowmen, not only do our deeds assist them, but we put our own problems in a fresher perspective. When we concern ourselves more with others, there is less time to be concerned with ourselves. In the midst of the miracle of serving, there is the promise of Jesus, that by losing ourselves, we find ourselves (see Matthew 10:39).

"Not only do we 'find' ourselves in terms of acknowledging guidance in our lives, but the more we serve our fellowmen in appropriate ways, the more substance there is to our souls. We become more significant individuals as we serve others. We become more substantive as we serve others—indeed, it is easier to 'find' ourselves because there is so much more of us to find."[16]

Perhaps the Savior gave the most important reason for service. It is that we can never know or be one with each other unless we serve one another. "For how knoweth a man the master whom he has not served, and who is a stranger unto him, and is far from the thoughts and intents of his heart?" (Mosiah 5:13).

We cannot satisfy our need to matter nor can we truly worship God without offering service. To His followers who were vying for prominent positions in His kingdom, the Savior taught, "Whosoever will be chief among you, let him be your servant" (Matthew 20:27). On a later occasion, He spoke of ministering to the needs of the hungry, the naked, the sick, and the imprisoned. He concluded His teaching with these words: "Verily I say unto you, Inasmuch as ye have done it unto one of the least of these my brethren, ye have done it unto me" (Matthew 25:40).

In latter-day revelation the Lord has instructed us to be "anxiously engaged in a good cause, and do many things of [our] own free will, and bring to pass much righteousness" (D&C 58:27). Service is an obligation of all members of the Church of Jesus Christ.

Sometimes it is mistakenly assumed that the most meaningful assignments are those that attract the greatest attention and recognition. However, the cheers from the crowd do not measure the importance of our service in the Lord's kingdom. It doesn't matter *where* you serve, it matters a great deal *how* you serve. One can get to heaven serving in the Primary just as fast as serving in the bishopric. Those who serve because they love the Lord are quite happy to serve inconspicuously since they know that compensation paid in the world's coin reduces the value of their service to God. In sum, our need to matter is met when we have and are committed to meaningful assignments of service.

The Need to Know

Finally, associated with man's sense of reason (represented by his mind) is his need to know the meaning of important truths. This need to know is satisfied by the "nourishing word of God" which helps man understand the connection between his choices and their consequences, between his choices in this life and the conditions of our next life, and the connection between our premortal life and our opportunities in this life.

The nourishing word of God provides meaningful connections between our choices and our becoming righteous. Indeed our knowing nourishing truths unlocks our moral agency. In the Garden of Eden before partaking of the fruit of the tree of knowledge of good and evil, Adam and Eve were innocent, but not righteous because they lacked the knowledge of their potential choices. Partaking of the fruit of the tree of knowledge gave them the knowledge they needed to choose between right and wrong and the opportunity to become righteous by choosing the right.

The condition of those who lacked knowing was vividly portrayed in Lehi and Nephi's dream of the tree of life. "And I saw numberless concourses of people, many of whom were pressing forward, that they might obtain the path which led unto the tree by which I stood. And it came to pass that they did come forth, and commence in the path which led to the tree. And it came to pass that there arose a mist of darkness; yea, even an exceedingly great mist of darkness, insomuch that they who had commenced in the path did lose their way, that they wandered off and were lost" (1 Nephi 8:21–23).

We have the need to know the way to the tree of life, a knowledge that is provided by the nurturing word of God that marks the path to the tree of life with these instructions: "Come and be baptized unto repentance, that ye also may be partakers of the fruit of the tree of life" (Alma 5:62).

The followers of Christ first gain a testimony of the gospel and then share it with others. Their testimony is that, "through the atonement of Jesus Christ, all mankind may be saved by obedience to the laws and ordinances of the gospel."[17] Those who listened to Alma and Amulek had a great question. Where is the nurturing word? They answered that the word is in Christ unto salvation. (see Alma 34:5–6)

We satisfy our need to know important truths when in the school of life we learn from the wisdom of others, from revelations from God, from our own experiences gained through making choices, and from personal study. We learn through each of our senses, each contributing to a deeper understanding of our relationship to Christ and how we can become more like Him.

The Need for Bread and Satan's Substitutes

In addition to our spiritual needs, we have physical needs represented symbolically by our need for "bread." All of God's children desire bread. After fasting for forty days, the Savior was both thirsty and hungry; He needed bread and water.

After Adam and Eve entered the lone and dreary world, they experienced the need for bread. God could have supplied Adam and Eve's bread, but instead He taught them that they should earn their bread by hard work. The reason He required them to earn their bread was so they could learn several important lessons.

The first lesson is that there is no free bread. Adam and Eve learned that if they wanted bread, then they must work hard to obtain it. We also need to work hard. Whenever we receive a blessing from God, it is because we keep the commandment on which it was based. As Adam and Eve worked for their living, they learned the law of the harvest—that which you sow, so shall ye reap.

The second lesson they were expected to learn was that after their best efforts to till the ground and plant and care for the seed, that God gives the harvest. We too depend on God's grace after all that we can do.

Finally, Adam and Eve were expected to learn to trust God that the harvest would be sufficient to supply the needs of all of God's children, and to spare—if they worked together and shared their surplus.

Bad Bread

Satan teaches three lies about bread. First, he teaches that man's need for bread is our most important need. Second, he teaches that all of our other needs can be satisfied with more bread. Finally, Satan teaches that there is not enough bread and we had better get as much as we can or go hungry. Understanding Satan's lies and the world's focus on bread helps us understand our sometimes misguided focus on getting and consuming more.

The Unpleasant Word of the World

Many believe that more bread is our most important need. These attempt to get more bread by substituting the pleasing word of man for the nurturing word of God. Nehor found a ready market for the false and pleasing word that there was no sin.

Nephi warned against those who attempt to substitute the pleasing word of man for the nurturing word of God in an attempt to get gain. "There shall be no priestcrafts; for, behold, priestcrafts are that men preach and set themselves up for a light unto the world, that they may get *gain* and *praise of the world*; but they seek not the welfare of Zion. Behold, the Lord hath forbidden this thing; wherefore, the Lord God hath given a commandment that all men should have charity, which charity is love. And except they should have charity they were nothing. Wherefore, if they should have charity they would not suffer the laborer in Zion to perish. But the laborer in Zion shall labor for Zion; for if they labor for money they shall perish" (2 Nephi 26:29–31; emphasis added).

Our needs for beauty, to belong, to matter, to know, and to have bread are interrelated. Bread is the staff of life and essential to sustain us. But a soul despairing for beauty, to belong, to matter, and bereft of nurturing beliefs either lacks a desire for bread and does not find it sustaining or overindulges in bread as a substitute for belonging, for being important, and for knowing. Thus, in a very real sense, all our needs are spiritual and cannot be arranged in some hierarchal order of importance. They are all important and must be satisfied simultaneously in the peaceful soul.

Perverted Assignments

With the focus on bread, assignments take on a perverse meaning. One perverse assignment is to earn more bread than the others. With this perverted assignment and our focus on earning the most bread, we worship things and other people who have succeeded in the bread market including those who can perform great physical acts of prowess from which they earn large sums of bread even when these same persons display great moral cowardice. So we have come to worship our overpaid athletes who often lack manners and decorum, but who can perform impressive physical feats. We are quite willing to ignore the moral misconduct of our political leaders as long as the economy is strong and the stock market is rising. And we too often keep silent on subjects that are morally wrong, but still legal.

Fickle Friends

Satan has substitutes for friends and belonging. He substitutes combinations that pursue only one purpose, to get more bread. Adam Smith, the eighteenth century moral philosopher commented that whenever business men get together, it is to collude and raise prices. But worse is what Satan has substituted for belonging—sex. The sale of this sacred symbol of the covenant of marriage, the plaguing sin of our generation, has spawned in its wake failed marriages, abortion, and abuse in families, confirming the gospel truth that unbridled passions lead to the inability to love and to belong.

Attempting to meet our needs for belonging, for caring, and for understanding with more bread was described by Anne Wilson Schaef. "We get so embroiled with possessions. We find ourselves feeling that we need to own places, persons, and things. We try to possess our lives, and we believe that we can. We need to learn from the butterfly that alights on our hand. If we watch it and admire it, as it chooses to stay for a while, we are blessed with its beauty. If we try to hold onto it, we will kill it." [18]

A wealthy man in our stake died recently. Most of those attending his funeral were not really his friends, but his wife's friends. Near the end of his life, this brother had considered being sealed to his wife in the temple. But by that time, his wife was not sure she wanted to spend eternity with him. So it never happened.

This man had accumulated lots of bread, a summer home in the mountains, a winter home in Florida, and a large permanent home where his wife lived. He also drove expensive cars. But this man died ignorant of nurturing truths, left few friends to mourn his passing, and never held a meaningful soul-saving assignment in the kingdom because he was too busy making money—a task which he performed very well. He believed as Korihor taught that "every man fared in this life according to the management of the creature; therefore every man prospered according to his genius, and that every man conquered according to his strength; and whatsoever a man did was no crime" (Alma 30:17).

○છ ౭౦

Monday night after family home evening and the children we in bed, John and Amy sat down with the checkbook. John earned an adequate salary, and some members of their ward considered them well-off. But the balance in their checkbook revealed financial pressures—a race between their money and the end of the month. John and Amy often wondered which would finish first.

Amy, who had a promising career before their marriage, offered without enthusiasm, "Well I could always go back to work." Then John responded, "I know there are families where mom and dad must both work to make ends meet. And maybe it works for families with older children. But for us right now, having mom at home is still more important than more money. So let's try a little harder to manage our money to the end of the month." Amy smiled gratefully at John and then wondered how she was going to feed her family during the last week of the month.

Conclusions

We all have the four basic needs. These needs can be satisfied through our four senses of at-one-ment that lead us to seek for beauty, for the love of friends, for meaningful assignments, and for the nourishing word—in ways that allow us to maintain our integrity, build Zion, and gain salvation. The alternative is to succumb to Satan's counterfeits and fulfill ourselves in ways that separate us from our best selves, from each other, and from the Lord's approval. Happiness comes from seeking to satisfy our needs in the Lord's way.

NOTES

1. Gordon B. Hinckley, "Every Convert Is Precious," *Liahona*, February 1999, 9.

2. Steven R. Covey, A. Roger Merrill, and Rebecca R. Merrill, *First Things First: To Live, to Love, to Learn, to Leave a Legacy*, First Fireside Edition, 1995.

3. *Collins English Dictionary,* 5th ed., 2000.

4. Gordon B. Hinckley, "I Believe," *Ensign,* August 1992, 2.

5. John H. Vandenberg, "My Brother's Keeper," *Ensign*, June 1971, 63.

6. "For the Beauty of the Earth," *Hymns of The Church of Jesus Christ of Latter-day Saints*, no. 92.

7. Richard G. Scott, "Finding Joy in Life," *Ensign,* May 1996, 24.

8. Pearl of Great Price; JSH 1:61.

9. Blum, Deborah. *Love at Goon Park: Harry Harlow and the Science of Affection*, (2002).

10. Clark Swain, "The Meaning of Love," *Ensign,* March 1972, 26.

11. hhtp://www.etymonline.com/index

12. Marvin J. Ashton, "What Is a Friend?" *Ensign,* January 1973, 41.

13. *For the Strength of Youth,* The Church of Jesus Christ of Latter-day Saints, (1990), 9.

14. Quoted by Kathleen H. Hughes, "What Greater Goodness Can We Know: Christlike Friends," *Ensign,* May 2005, 74.

15. "Each Life That Touches Ours for Good," *Hymns of The Church of Jesus Christ of Latter-day Saints,* no. 293.

16. Spencer W. Kimball (1895–1985), *Ensign,* December 1974, 2.

17. The Pearl of Great Price, "The Articles of Faith of the Church of Jesus Christ of Latter-day Saints," 60–61.

18. Anne Wilson Schaef, *Meditations for Women Who Do Too Much*, (May 1990), 184.

Chapter Eight

A ZION ORGANIZATION

A quorum is three things: first, a class; second,
a fraternity; and third, a service unit.[1]
—Stephen L. Richards

෨ ෩

As John entered his elders quorum class, he was greeted warmly by several of his brothers with whom he exchanged some light-hearted banter. After calling the quorum together, quorum president Andy Doering turned the time for the lesson over to quorum instructor Ted Smart. The lesson that week was on justification and sanctification. It was evident as the lesson progressed that Brother Smart was well prepared to instruct his brethren.

At the end of the lesson, Wilbur asked a question that changed the whole course of the lesson. Wilbur commented, "I have listened with great interest to the lesson. The thought has crossed my mind that we will soon forget today's lesson if we do not find application to what we have learned."

Then Wilbur explained his recent experience with a ward member. The nonmember husband of one of the elderly members of the ward had passed away. Wilbur said he visited the widow and offered his sympathy. Leaving the home after the visit, his eyes wandered over their home. It was in need of much care—the gardens needed weeding, the lawn needed mowing. But most of all, the roof of the house needed repairs. Wilbur had wondered to himself, *How would this sister cope with the sudden problems now falling upon her?* "She needs help!" he exclaimed to no one in particular.

Finally, Wilbur proposed to the group that they make an application of the principle that was being taught—by working with the widow to maintain her home. The elders agreed and spent the balance of the meeting on organizing the project to assist her. The roof project was a perfect application for the day's lesson.

John reflected to himself as he left the classroom, *There was a good feeling among us today. This project is just what we needed to get this quorum working together again. A lesson had been taught, a brotherhood had been strengthened, and a service project had been organized to assist someone in need.* [2]

Three Fundamental Needs

John's quorum meeting addressed three of man's fundamental needs. These three needs include *love* from a friend, a sense of *worth* gained from meaningful assignments to serve others, and *truth* found in the nourishing word of God. To assist His children satisfy their needs in the right way, God has provided an organizational template exemplified by priesthood quorums in which these needs can be satisfied. The template illustrated by priesthood quorums can be applied to other organizational units, including wards, communities, and the most important of all organizations, families.

The model organization includes a class where members are nourished by the good word of God, a brotherhood (or sisterhood) when members feel loved, and a service organization where members' need to matter is satisfied by a meaningful assignment. When units are properly organized, they not only satisfy man's basic needs for at-one-ment, but they create the at-one-ment described in the scriptures as Zion.

A Class and Becoming of One Mind

The purpose of a class is to satisfy one's need for truth or the nourishing word of God. Then as class members are nourished by the good word of God, they come to an at-one-ment of understanding—they become of one mind.

Sister Virginia H. Pearce once described the effects on a fifteen-year-old boy of two different classroom experiences. One experience contributed to his separation from the Church. His other classroom experience led to his unity with the Church and its members.

> The young man recounted, "When I was about 15, I started to have a lot of questions about the Church. I thought maybe there would be a chance to talk about my questions at church, but it didn't happen. In priesthood it seemed like most of the time everybody talked about the game the night before. Sunday School was about the same—maybe a little lesson thrown in during the last five minutes where the teacher asked questions, and it was kind of 'guess-the-right-answer-from-the-manual-time.'"

> Well, other things happened—late Saturday nights, a switch to an earlier meeting schedule—and soon the young man's attendance dropped to nothing. Several years passed by until he found himself in church again. This time his face lit up as he described his Sunday School class.

> "The teacher was this unimpressive-looking guy, but he was so excited about what he was teaching. He didn't waste a minute. He asked important questions. Everyone had their scriptures. They looked up verses. Shared ideas. They listened to each other. They talked about problems at school and how they fit in with the lesson. You could tell that the people in the class were all different, but they had one amazing thing in common—they

were all interested in learning the gospel. After five minutes, I knew that this was a good place for me."[3]

The Lord enjoined the saints to hold classes and to teach one another the doctrine. The Lord revealed to Joseph Smith, "And as all have not faith, seek ye diligently and teach one another words of wisdom; yea, seek ye out of the best books words of wisdom; seek learning, even by study and also by faith" (D&C 88:118).

H. Aldridge Gillespie of the Seventy taught that classes that focus on the nourishing word of God create unity. "If our wards and branches are to be spared the divisive influence that has been the downfall of many people, we must avoid the foolishness and precepts of men when teachers and speakers do not focus on 'the counsel of God, for they set it aside, supposing they know of themselves' (see 2 Nephi 9:28). On many such occasions, 'they teach for doctrines the commandments of men, having a form of godliness, but they deny the power thereof' (JS—H 1:19)."[4]

President Harold B. Lee described the ideal class in this way: "We are not set apart to teach philosophies or sciences of the world. We are set apart to teach the principles of the gospel as found in the four standard works....We are convinced that our members are hungry for the gospel, undiluted, with its abundant truths and insights."[5]

When classes focus on true doctrine revealed by God to His prophets, then an at-one-ment of understanding and a unity of the faith can result. Paul taught that "[God] gave some, apostles; and some, prophets; and some, evangelists; and some, pastors and teachers; for the perfecting of the saints, for the work of the ministry, for the edifying of the body of Christ: till we all come in the unity of the faith, and of the knowledge of the Son of God, unto a perfect man, unto the measure of the stature of the fulness of Christ" (Ephesians 4:11–13).

Elder L. Tom Perry counseled, "Brethren, let us make of our quorums a class where we will receive the best instruction possible to guide us in our responsibilities and obligations as bearers of His holy priesthood."[6] If priesthood quorums (and other organizations) followed Elder Perry's counsel, their class members would come to understand alike and be of *one mind.*

Priesthood quorums can be an effective means for meeting quorum members' need to know if they focus on sharing the good word of God. Of course, quorum instruction does not substitute for personal study and prayer, yet priesthood classes can be an effective means for confirming understanding, answering questions, and strengthening convictions through the bearing of pure testimony.

A Brotherhood and Becoming of One Heart

Consider the second characteristic of a priesthood quorum—a fraternity or brotherhood. The purpose of a fraternity is to meet its members' need for love and belonging. A properly functioning unit not only meets its members' need for love, but creates an at-one-ment of affection described in the scriptures as an at-one-ment of hearts.

Aristotle wrote that friendship is a single soul dwelling in two bodies. The scriptures describe just such a friendship—"the soul of Jonathan was knit with the soul of David, and Jonathan loved him as his own soul" (1 Samuel 18:1). The evidence of their friendship was Jonathan's repeated efforts to reconcile his father Saul to David and when reconciliation between the two was impossible, Jonathan shielded David from danger.[7] Friendship, a single soul dwelling in several bodies describes well a quorum brotherhood, a relief society, a family, or a ward where the members are of "one heart."

A Service Organization and No Poor among Them

The third characteristic of a priesthood quorum is service. A service organization is one that organizes the efforts of its members to provide helpful activities. If the service project is properly organized, members feel a sense of worth because they have opportunities to serve those in need.

One outcome of this righteous service can be the elimination of poverty—so that "there are no poor among them." But teaching the gospel is also a service that may eliminate the poverty of understanding. And offering brotherly love may also be a service that eliminates the poverty of love.

The service that matters most, and the one best designed to confirm that we matter, is the service that brings souls to Christ (see D&C 16:6). Of course this service may take many forms, including the repair of a widow's leaking roof. But in all acts of service to God's children we will come to know that we matter because we will earn the Savior's approbation: "Inasmuch as ye have done it unto one of the least of these my brethren, ye have done it unto me" (Matthew 25:40).

Everyone needs to feel that he or she is an integral part of the ward; unity and perfection come through involvement in the ministry. President Gordon B. Hinckley taught that every new convert needs a Church responsibility. This may suggest that without the opportunity to be part of the Lord's work, the perfecting and edifying process is incomplete, and a precious soul may be lost. [8]

Whether our service is to our fellowmen or to God, it is the same (see Mosiah 2:17). If we love God, we should keep His commandments and feed His sheep (see John 21:16–17). Finally, the objects of our service must be those in need. Indeed, "Pure religion and undefiled before God and the Father is this, to visit the fatherless and widows in their affliction, and to keep himself unspotted from the world" (James 1:27). Successful service then is characterized by the alleviation of poverty of spirit and body until there are no poor among us.

Organizational Interdependence

While the three dimensions of an ideally organized priesthood quorum, Relief Society, family, or ward have been discussed independent of each other, it must be clear that all three dimensions are interdependent. A class cannot function properly without brotherhood among its members and a point to each lesson—the point being that the lesson prepares class members to serve.

A brotherhood cannot function well unless class members have an opportunity to serve, for charity without service is like faith without works—dead. Furthermore, unless we know how to serve, even if we have desires to serve, we are unlikely to render effective service. Finally, service rendered without caring is forced labor and availeth little. These interdependencies between the three dimensions of a properly organized unit are summarized below and in the table that follows.

A Class and a Service Organization

A useful class must lead to changes in the lives of the participants, including changes in behavior. President Boyd K. Packer taught, "True doctrine, understood, changes attitudes and behavior. The study of the doctrines of the gospel will improve behavior quicker than a study of behavior will improve behavior."[9] Indeed, an ideal class should lead naturally to an application of the principles taught—to a meaningful assignment.

On the other hand, few if any skills can be learned without application. Thus, service projects can often serve as an ideal class. In my case, I learned to paint, repair roofs, pour cement, and perform basic wiring as a member of an elders quorum in Dale City,

Virginia—skills unlikely to be learned if the training were limited to a formal classroom.

A Class and a Brotherhood

The success of a class depends on the teacher caring for the students and of the students loving their teacher in return. One summary statement of this need for students to know that their teacher cares is, "We don't care how much you know, until we know how much you care."[10]

The Lord confirmed that our influence must be powered by love. "No power or influence can or ought to be maintained by virtue of the priesthood, only by persuasion, by long-suffering, by gentleness and meekness, and by love unfeigned" (D&C 121:41).

President Joseph F. Smith summarized the connection between love and learning. "You will observe that the most potent influence over the mind of a child to persuade it to learn, to progress, or to accomplish anything is the influence of love. More can be accomplished for good by unfeigned love, in bringing up a child, than by any other influence that can be brought to bear upon it. A child that cannot be conquered by the lash, or subdued by violence, may be controlled in an instant by unfeigned affection and sympathy. I know this is true; and this principle prevails in every condition of life."[11]

Learning and being loved are interdependent. We learn best from those whom we feel truly care about us. I trace my interest in agricultural economics to Professor Ernest M. Morrison who took an interest in me as a beginning student at Utah State University. Needing employment after my mission, I wrote to him and asked if he remembered me and if it might be possible for me to continue grading papers for him after I returned to school? He wrote me back the following: "While I wouldn't want to do so, I could pick your hide out in a tannery and yes you can have your job back."

With such encouragement from a friend, my lifelong interest in agricultural economics was assured.

A Brotherhood and a Service Organization

Joseph Smith demonstrated the importance of combining charity with service. One time the prophet was with some members of the Church when he learned that a brother's house had been burned by enemies. When Church members said they felt sorry for him, the Prophet took some money from his pocket and said, "I feel sorry for this brother to the amount of five dollars. How much do you...feel sorry [for him]?"[12]

There may be many motives for service, including the desire for personal gain and recognition. But the Prophet Moroni taught that if our works are to be credited for good, they must be done for the right reasons. "If a man offereth a gift, or prayeth unto God, except he shall do it with real intent it profiteth him nothing. For behold, it is not counted unto him for righteousness" (Moroni 7:6–7).

Confirming the importance of service with love, the Apostle Paul taught that the more excellent motive for service is because of brotherhood or charity (see 1 Corinthians 12:31). "Though I speak with the tongues of men and of angels, and have not charity, I am become as sounding brass, or a tinkling cymbal.... And though I bestow all my goods to feed the poor...and have not charity, it profiteth me nothing" (1Corinthians 13:1, 3).

If our service is to be most effective, it must be accomplished for the love of God and the love of His children. The Savior applied that principle in the Sermon on the Mount, in which He commanded us to love our enemies, bless them that curse us, do good to them that hate us, and pray for them that despitefully use us and persecute us (see Matthew 5:44). He explained the purpose of that commandment as follows: "For if ye love them which love you, what reward have ye? do not even the publicans the same? And if ye salute your brethren only, what do ye more than others? do not even the publicans so?" (Matthew 5:46–47).

Elder Dallin H. Oaks taught the principle "that our service should be for the love of God and the love of fellowmen rather than for personal advantage or any other lesser motive—is admittedly a high standard. The Savior must have seen it so, since he joined his commandment for selfless and complete love directly with the ideal of perfection. The very next verse of the Sermon on the Mount contains this great commandment: 'Be ye therefore perfect, even as your Father which is in heaven is perfect' (Matthew 5:48)." [13] Thus, a brotherhood without service or service without brotherhood is incomplete.

Zion in the Family

A quorum properly organized into a class, a brotherhood, and a service unit will successfully lead its members to a shared understanding, hearts knit together in love, and loving service that eliminates poverty. Finally, if such a wonderful organization can create at-one-ment and Zion in a priesthood quorum, why not follow the same organization and create Zion in our families?

Instead of a priesthood class, we organize family home evenings, read the scriptures together as a family, and use other family gatherings to teach one another to become a family of one mind. We love one another, find joy in each other's success, and share their disappointment when they fail.

In a Zion family, we share and serve so that there are no poor among us. In a Zion family, we love each other and feel love in return. We express this love and feeling of belonging by attending church together, celebrating important events together, especially events in which members of the family are featured. Furthermore, we are also there to comfort the discouraged. The result is that in such a properly organized family, all members are of one heart.

Lastly, every member of the family has a meaningful assignment. Members of the family are neither guests nor strangers, but family. In such a condition each provides service to the extent of their capabilities so that by equally sharing in the responsibilities and rewards of family-hood, there are no poor (nor rich) among us.

A Zion Organization that Meets Our Needs

The table that follows describes how a properly organized priesthood quorum (or family) meets the needs of its members. Numbers in the text correspond to numbered cells in the table.

The Need for Truth

1. Truth has a familiar ring and leads to an agreement among the sincere seekers of truth. When true doctrine is taught in our quorums we become of one mind.

2. However, the effectiveness of the class in nurturing its members with the good word of God will be negated unless a true spirit of brotherhood exists in the quorum. Indeed, the truism mentioned previously still applies. "I don't care how much you know unless I know you care." The good word of God becomes nurturing in the presence of true brotherhood where each member of the quorum seeks the interests of his quorum members.

3. Finally, no learning or nurturing by the good word of God will be long remembered or even completely understood unless it is applied. Thus, instruction with opportunities to apply one's knowledge in rendering service is the most effective means of truly being nurtured with the good word of God.

The outcome of proper priesthood organization that provides a class, a brotherhood, and service opportunities is to dissolve disagreements and erase confusion so that the quorum is of *one mind*.

The Need to Belong

4. The feelings of belonging and the sensation of friendship are best discovered in classes that emphasize the love of the Savior— that God so loved the world and each one of us that He sent His only Begotten Son to the world to ransom fallen man. When we gain an understanding of God's great plan of happiness, we learn to love God and man because He first loved us.

5. When we come to understand and feel the great love the Father and the Son have for each of us, we become less concerned about being loved, as we are concerned about expressing love to other members of the quorum. In particular, the quorum becomes sensitive to those most in need of caring.

6. To properly express caring, quorum members organize to meet the needs of their members. Sometimes these needs are physical. Most of the time they are spiritual, including the need to belong and feel loved.

When quorum members truly feel loved and are filled with a love for others in their quorum, they have become of *one heart.*

The Need to Matter

7. A proper priesthood class meets its members' need to matter by instructing them on their relationship to God. The fundamental lesson is that we matter, not so much by what we have done, al-though this is important, but by who and whose we are.

8. Priesthood quorum members come to believe that they matter when they serve. In addition they believe they matter when they learn they are loved by God and by those who have been called of God to hold His priesthood.

9. Only as we strive to bring souls to Christ can we truly feel that we matter because we are performing the service that matters most to God. Of course this service may take many forms. But

in all acts of service to God's children we will come to know we matter because we serve those whom God loves.

Finally, the righteous works of quorum members that validate their need to matter are directed toward those whose needs are greatest—the poor among us including the poor in understanding, the poor in social graces, the poorly dressed, and the poor who lack life's basic necessities. As a result of righteous works of service there are *fewer poor among us than before.*

ଔ ∽

John watched Sam Synder in amazement. Sam was clearly at home on Widow Losely's roof. He moved with purpose and without fear, laying down and nailing shingles in one effortless movement. Other members of the quorum—appearing to lack assignments—he directed to bring shingles to the roof, to remove and place old shingles in trash containers, and all the time smiling as if roofing on a hot day was the most fun a person could ask for. John asked Sam, "Where did you learn your roofing skills?" "Well, I started out helping my dad fix our roof and just moved on from there. I enjoyed it and was good at it…and ended up paying for my mission by roofing houses."

Later on, John reflected on the roofing experience. *There was a different feeling between us today. And I will never again see Sam—"Spiderman"* [as he became known that day]—*as weak and shy. Indeed,* John thought, *if our project had a hero, it was Sam.* And in that moment, John wondered if the service project motivated by their caring for Sister Losely had led the quorum to experience something like Zion—where for a while, on the roof, there was no distinction between quorum members based on profession, learning, positions held, or income. They were just brothers trying to help Widow Losely.

Summary—Building Zion

"And the Lord called his people ZION, because they were of one heart and one mind, and dwelt in righteousness; and there was no poor among them" (Moses 7:18).

Organization of a Quorum (& family)	THE NEEDS OF QUORUM (AND FAMILY) MEMBERS		
	To Know the Truth	The Need to Love and Be Loved	The Need to Matter
Class	1. Quorum classes focus on true doctrines that nourish class members with the good word of God.	4. Quorum classes educate not only the minds, but the hearts of its members. Thus quorum members are better equipped to fellowship others and to be fellowshipped in return.	7. Quorum classes increase their members' capacities to render meaningful service by educating their hands and feet. They are taught how, when, why, and whom to serve, both inside and outside of the chapel.
Brotherhood	2. Quorum members learn best from those who care about them. "I don't care how much you know until I know how much you care" describes the importance of love between students and teachers.	5. The quorum becomes a brother-hood as members learn to care for each other and to feel cared for in return.	8. The meaningfulness of quorum service is increased because it is performed by one brother for another.
Service Unit	3. Some lessons can only be learned through experience. Thus, classes direct quorum members toward meaningful assignments that complement the lessons learned in the classes.	6. We experience brotherhood more intensively when we serve together and each other.	9. Quorum members sense their self-worth as they perform righteous service, eliminating poverty and inequality among themselves.
Zion: result of a properly organized priesthood quorum (& family)	Quorum members have their need to know satisfied by the nourishing word of God, and they become *of one mind.*	Quorum members have their need for love and belonging satisfied by their brotherhood, and they become *of one heart.*	Quorum members feel that they matter as they perform meaningful service, and they eliminate poverty among those in need. The result is that there are *no poor among them.*

NOTES

1. Stephen L. Richards in Conference Report, Oct. 1938, 118; quoted by L. Tom Perry, "What Is a Quorum?" *Ensign*, November 2004, 23.

2. Adapted from an address by L. Tom Perry, "When Ye Are Prepared, Ye Shall Not Fear," *Ensign, November 1981, 37.*

3. Virginia H. Pearce, "The Ordinary Classroom—a Powerful Place for Steady and Continued Growth," *Ensign, November 1996, 11.*

4. H. Aldridge Gillespie, "Be Ye One," *Ensign, June 2004, 56.*

5. *Teachings of Presidents of the Church: Harold B. Lee*, (2000), 65.

6. L. Tom Perry, "When Ye Are Prepared, Ye Shall Not Fear," *Ensign, November 1981, 37.*

7. Jeffrey R. Holland, "Real Friendship," *New Era, June 1998, 62.*

8. H. Aldridge Gillespie, "Be Ye One," *Ensign, June 2004, 56.*

9. Boyd K. Packer, "Little Children," *Ensign,* November 1986, 16.

10. Quoted by Theo E. McKean, "To Love Is to Understand," *Tambuli, July 1977, 33.*

11. Joseph F. Smith. Conference Report, October 1902, 92.

12. Hyrum L. Andrus and Helen Mae Andrus, comps., *They Knew the Prophet*, (1974), 150.

13. Dallin H. Oaks, "Why Do We Serve?" *New Era, March 1988, 5.*

Chapter Nine

At-one-ment, Order, and Beauty

Organize yourselves; prepare every needful thing;
and establish a house, even a house of prayer, a house
of fasting, a house of faith, a house of learning, a house
of glory, a house of order, a house of God.
—D&C 88:119

૨જ ৪৩

Amy answered the phone. It was Molly confirming their visiting teaching appointment with Missy Williams for that afternoon. John would be home early from work to watch the children so Amy agreed to their visit. Molly stopped by as planned at 3:00 p.m. and soon enough they were at the Williams home. Amy steeled herself for the experience. It wasn't meeting with Sister Williams that Amy dreaded. Sister Williams was always pleasant enough. It was the mess and disorganization at the Williams home that left Amy feeling weighed down after each of their visits.

The first sights that greeted Amy as she stepped out of Molly's car were the deflated soccer balls and bleached plastic toys partially hidden in the dirt and weeds where once a lawn had thrived. Then she noticed the old car in the driveway that brother Williams said he intended to restore one day. While waiting for repairs, the old car appeared to have become a storage unit, filled with who knows what. Behind the car waiting for repairs, the half-open garage door revealed an assortment of power tools, partially-filled cardboard boxes, used sports gear, and clutter—all preventing cars from being parked in their spaces.

The Williams home could have been, perhaps once was, a respectable looking abode. Now, however, the house needed painting, the drains needed to be reconnected, and the curled shingles could only be counted on for another year or two to prevent water damage to the interior of the house. In summary, the house had a pitiful appearance that made Amy wince when her friends connected the Williams family to the Church.

Sister Williams greeted them amiably at the front door and invited them into her home. She made some comment that could have been taken for an apology for the clutter in her home. "Sorry things are so messy," she lamented, "I just can't keep up with everything and the kids." Then she ordered her two youngest children to turn off the TV and made a place for Amy and Molly to sit down by pushing her dog off his comfortable "bed" on the coach and picking up several plates with very dried pizza crusts on them.

Amy looked around and noted the washed and wrinkled clothes in a heap covering the dining room table. From where she sat, she could see piles of dirty dishes littering counter tops and the sink. The vacuum cleaner stood at attention in the middle of the floor, but the dirt on the carpet suggested it had been unemployed for some time.

Amy felt revolted by the disarray, dirt, and disorganization in this household. She was sorry to admit it, but the disorder in the Williams home created some emotional distance between her and Sister Williams. In an unguarded moment, she thought to herself, *If we both make it to Zion, I hope we're not neighbors.* And then she immediately felt guilty for such unkind feelings toward the Williams family.

The Need for Beauty and Order

We all have a spiritual need for beauty. We satisfy our need for beauty by creating order in our lives and in our surroundings.

When we are confronted by ugliness as Amy was during her visit to the Williams family, our spiritual senses are offended. Moreover, often too much exposure to the ugly can desensitize us to the point that we first, endure it, then pity ourselves because of it, and then ignore the litter in our lives.

God intended to help us satisfy our need for beauty when He organized the world by converting chaos into order.[1] We follow God's example when we create order in our own lives. Bathsheba Smith, the wife of George A. Smith, provides an example of an ordered life.

"On her last day in Nauvoo, Bathsheba tidied up her home, swept the floor, put the broom in its accustomed place behind the door, and then stepped outside to a waiting wagon, leaving behind rooms full of beloved items and a house ready for occupancy by strangers." Elder Gerald Lund asked, "I have wondered what kind of woman would walk away from her home, leaving it to her enemies and be sure it is swept clean before she does so."[2] The answer is a woman who loved the beauty found in an ordered life.

Order is a condition of at-one-ment in which things and people are in their proper relationships to each other—a condition of at-one-ment in which all things are arranged logically, comprehensibly, or naturally.[3] In the world of reason, we find beauty in organized ideas. In the world of music we find beauty in soul stirring melodies. In the world of plants, we find beauty in their balance of colors and location in space. And in our homes we find beauty where things are cared for, and everything has a place—and when not in use is in its place.

Our innate need for beauty leads us to seek for order and at-one-ment with our surroundings. To help us gain this at-one-ment, beauty, and order we should learn from the process the Gods followed when they organized the world. By following their example, we too can create order and beauty in our surroundings.

In the beginning, God observed matter unorganized and organized it into a world by placing the elements and all created things in their proper relationship to each other. Order and beauty is not the natural state of our world. Energy, both spiritual and physical, is required to convert disorder and disarray into order and beauty. The power to create order and beauty comes from Christ's Atonement through which we can overcome our disconnections caused by sin and the natural dissolution inherent in the universe (sometimes described as the second law of thermodynamics—which explains why you may see a drinking glass fall and shatter into disorganized pieces, but you will never witness the process reversed).

Just as the Lord created order in the world, we are instructed to do the same in our sphere of influence. The Savior admonished, "Organize yourselves; prepare every needful thing; and establish a house, even a house of prayer, a house of fasting, a house of faith, a house of learning, a house of glory, a house of *order*, a house of God" (D&C 88:119; emphasis added). Elsewhere the Lord declared, "Behold, mine house is a house of order, saith the Lord God and not a house of confusion" (D&C 132:8). And we are to do all things in wisdom and order that we should not run faster than we have strength lest disorder follow.

In the spirit of "[likening] all scriptures unto us, that it might be for our profit and learning" (1 Nephi 19:23), what follows are ten suggestions for bringing organization and beauty into our lives and our homes, into our work, our play, our gospel assignments, and our families. These suggestions originate from the teachings about the organization of this world when God rescued order from disorder.

The organizational lessons are so important that when Ammon brought the gospel to King Lamoni, he began by teaching him about the Creation. The importance of the Creation or organizational lessons is also emphasized by their inclusion in temple ordinances and in the Pearl of Great Price and the Bible. From these repeated references to the organization of the world, we might infer that the Lord has a message for us. The lesson is that we are to create our own world of order and beauty by following His example.

Ten Steps to Order and At-one-ment

1. Begin with a Goal

Order begins with a vision expressed as a goal. God began the Creation by identifying a goal. It was, He declared, His work and His glory to bring to pass the immortality and eternal life of man (see Moses 1:39). Heavenly Father taught us a great lesson when He selected our progress and happiness as His goal. The lesson is that our work and glory, like that of the Father, is to assist in bringing to pass the eternal life of man by helping others find their proper relationship to God.

Establishing a goal creates order and at-one-ment in at least five different ways. A goal is an expression of our faith, which is based on strong desires to obtain an object and a belief that one's goal can be achieved. What distinguishes faith from day dreams? When we have faith, desires and beliefs are sufficiently strong that we work to achieve our goal. And in the process of believing, desiring, and working, one creates order.

Second, goals provide a criterion for choice. All of us face alternative choices, and unless we have a goal, we have no basis for deciding among our alternatives. We are like Alice in Wonderland who faced a choice between paths, but had no goal to direct the recommendation of the wise Cheshire Cat. However, with a goal, we can order our lives through wise choices—those alternatives most likely to lead us to the desired end.

Third, goals order our relationships with others. Once others know our goals they can offer to lead and lift us to our desired end. Our goals become the trumpet that calls others to the battle. For example, Chief Captain Moroni regained order among the Nephites by establishing a goal of liberty. Then the people, informed of his worthy goal, rallied to his aid.

Fourth, goals also order our relationship to God by giving us a focus for our prayers and a specific request for a blessing that God can answer. God cannot answer a fuzzy prayer that is not focused on a clear, obtainable, and measurable goal. Goals give clarity and order to what we desire the Lord to do.

Fifth, and lastly, goals give us order in our lives by giving us a measure against which our efforts can be compared. Comparing where we are to our goals answers the question, are we creating by our acts what we envisioned spiritually?

2. Convene a Council and Agree on a Plan

Order requires agreement and commitment. So the second step in the ordering effort we call the Creation was to call a council. So, in the beginning, God convened a premortal council during which we agreed to support our Father's plan for our happiness with its goal of our immortality and eternal life.

There were, I'm sure, multitudes of interesting and important things to discuss at this council, but the goal of eternal life and immortality for the children of men captured the agenda. The second characteristic of this premortal council was its openness. All were allowed to express their opinion. However, not all were to speak at once. "Appoint among yourselves a teacher, and let not all be spokesmen at once; but let one speak at a time and let all listen unto his sayings, that when all have spoken that all may be edified of all, and that every man may have an equal privilege" (D&C 88:122).

Another important characteristic of the premortal council was that it included the adoption of and our commitment to a plan for achieving the goal. A goal answers the question, what is to be achieved? A plan for achieving our goal answers the questions, by whom, by what means, where, and when. A proper plan helps us avoid the duplication of effort, assures that important efforts will be made, helps us cooperate by assuring that our efforts are synergistic, and eliminates our blaming each other for failure. The plan to achieve the goal of eternal life and immortality is sometimes referred to as the plan of happiness. The reason that progress toward Godhood and happiness are the same goal is because man is only happy as he progresses toward perfect order.

Finally, one of the most important characteristics of this council was the demonstration of the Father and the Son's divine love. Love is required for all successful councils because it leads to unity. Its alternative, selfishness, always leads to division and disorder. Because of their selfish desires to rule that disconnected them from others in the council, it was inevitable that Satan and his followers would reject the Father's plan. They did and were separated from His kingdom to begin their work of disordering. But the rest of us remained. We agreed on the goal of immortality and eternal life. We accepted our responsibilities contained in the plan just as the Savior accepted His redeeming responsibility. Indeed, our consent to the goal and the plan was more than mere agreement. The scriptures record that we accepted God's plan of happiness and our responsibilities with shouts of joy.

Later on in the Garden of Eden we learned just how important councils can be. In the first case, Eve, acting without Adam's counsel, was deceived by Satan. On her own, she decided to partake of the fruit of the tree of knowledge of good and evil, perhaps recognizing that someone needed to break the impasse between innocence in the Garden and mortality and progress outside the Garden. In the second case, before consulting with Eve, Adam intended to remain alone in the Garden of Eden and frustrate the plan of happiness. Fortunately, Adam counseled with Eve who helped him see the need to also partake of the fruit. Eve's wise counsel saved them both from separateness.

3. Meaningful Separations

Meaning comes from placing objects in their proper place and relationship to each other. Of course, this means that everything has a place. One way we find places for things is by placing similar things together and separating them from those things that are different.

God exemplified the meaningful separations principle. For example, He separated the light from the darkness, the land from the water, one season from another, and He separated animals and plants that were similar from those that were different.

Just as God separated night from day, so can we. For us, our days begin when we wake up. If this event is without order, disorder reigns. Successful missionaries I know have disciplined themselves to separate day from night by always getting up on or before the time set in their mission. The Lord emphasized the importance of our separating days from nights when He commanded, "Cease to be idle; cease to be unclean; cease to find fault one with another; cease to sleep longer than is needful; retire to thy bed early, that ye may not be weary; arise early, that your bodies and your minds may be invigorated" (D&C 88:124).

There are many other separations that will bring order into our lives and our homes. One is to separate the Sabbath day from the other days of the week. "For in six days the Lord made heaven and earth, and the sea, and all that in them is; wherefore the Lord blessed the Sabbath day, and hallowed it" (Mosiah 13:19). Another meaningful separation is between tithes and offerings—that are the Lord's—and our other resources.

When the influence of the wicked threatens to overpower the will of the righteous, God commands His people to separate, to flee from the wicked. So the children of Israel fled Egypt. Lot and his family fled Sodom and Gomorrah. And Lehi and his family fled from Jerusalem. In our time we separate ourselves from evil influences by choosing our friends from among the faithful, by listening to and watching only uplifting entertainment.

Making our houses places of order means separating out from other times, a time to study, to pray, to counsel together as families, a time to eat together, and a time to play together. Perhaps one of the most complete instruction manuals on meaningful separations is found in Ecclesiastes.

> A time to be born, and a time to die; a time to plant, and a time to pluck up that which is planted;
>
> A time to kill, and a time to heal; a time to break down, and a time to build up;
>
> A time to weep, and a time to laugh; a time to mourn, and a time to dance;
>
> A time to cast away stones, and a time to gather stones together; a time to embrace, and a time to refrain from embracing;
>
> A time to get, and a time to lose; a time to keep, and a time to cast away;
>
> A time to rend, and a time to sew; a time to keep silence, and a time to speak;
>
> A time to love, and a time to hate; a time of war, and a time of peace. [Ecclesiastes 3:2–8]

4. Prioritization

Another way the Lord rescued order from the clutches of chaos during the Creation was by prioritizing His creative acts. First, He organized matter into an earth. Then He separated the land from the water and the light from darkness. Next He planted seeds from which grew grasses, shrubs, and trees. Then He brought forth animal life. And finally, He brought forth man. Any reversal of priorities in the Creation would have caused disaster and disorder. Surely the animals couldn't have survived without the grasses and other plants on which they depended for their food. The plants, shrubs, and grasses, meanwhile, could not have existed if first the land and water had not been separated.

As a practical matter, those things of highest priority are those most likely to help us achieve our most important goal—exaltation and eternal life for us and our family and friends. So we prioritize by asking what will be of most worth to me and others in our quest to become more like God? What can I do which will last the longest? What is most Christlike? What things must be done first?

5. Proper Identification

One of Adam's first assignments from the Lord was to name the animals. While such an assignment may seem trivial, proper identification is an essential part of creating order. Indeed Satan attempts to destroy order by confusing us by calling evil good and good evil. Through the prophet Isaiah, the Lord warned, "Wo unto them that call evil good, and good evil, that put darkness for light, and light for darkness, that put bitter for sweet, and sweet for bitter! Wo unto the wise in their own eyes and prudent in their own sight!" (2 Nephi 15:20–21).

6. Neither Is the Man without the Woman nor the Woman without the Man

The crowning act of creation was the union of Adam and Eve. It was not good for Adam or Eve to be alone. God made clear the importance of the connections between Adam and Eve and husbands and wives when He commanded them to love each other with all their hearts, a connection similarly commanded to be made with God. From the Creation we learn that the proper relationship between the man and the woman is as husband and wife.

By making the creation of Adam and Eve and their proper relationship to each other and to Himself the crowning event of His Creation, God signaled the pre-eminent role of the family and its most important place in His house of order. We have been counseled that no other success can compensate for failure in the home. Yet, so many demands on our time try to cut in line in front of the family. The correlation efforts of the Church are designed to maintain the priority focus of the family. Family councils, family prayer, family home evening, family history centers, and the recent proclamation on the family all remind us of the priority position of the family.

7. Provide Needed Resources, Opportunities, and Training

An important lesson learned from God's Creation was His providing Adam and Eve and their posterity the resources they needed for success. God created the earth whereupon He placed man. Then He gave man the opportunity to choose between alternatives because righteousness required that we have choices to make. Finally, He organized the world so that Adam and Eve could learn that work precedes rewards, and if they were to have food, they must till the earth. God also gave them commandments and taught them to pray and make covenants which when kept would bring blessings. God also has sent prophets among the children of men to instruct them. In our days, we have the written word and regular messages from the General Authorities of the Church. For auxiliary leaders and teachers, there are manuals, teacher development classes, and leaders to consult.

When the Savior visited the Nephites, He expressed His concern for their physical as well as their spiritual well-being. He asked if there were any who were sick, halt, or blind and then healed them. Imagine the difference in their learning capacities when their physical as well as their spiritual needs were addressed.

One of the most important resources God gave to Adam and Eve and their descendants was His example. In creating man, God demonstrated the principle of order. He created order by following a pattern. This example was Himself, "And I, God, said unto mine Only Begotten, which was with me from the beginning: Let us make man in our image, after our likeness; and it was so" (Moses 2:26). Prophets provide us a pattern. So do our leaders and parents. We read the scriptures to find proper patterns. The life of the Savior was a model for us to follow.

8. Obey the Lord to "Come unto Me"

While in the Garden of Eden, Adam and Eve were in the presence of the Lord. After they were cast out of the Garden of Eden, they were commanded to keep in contact and to receive His instructions through prayer.

"And Adam and Eve, his wife, called upon the name of the Lord, and they heard the voice of the Lord from the way toward the Garden of Eden, speaking unto them, and they saw him not; for they were shut out from his presence. And he gave unto them commandments, that they should worship the Lord their God, and should offer the firstlings of their flocks, for an offering unto the Lord. And Adam was obedient unto the commandments of the Lord" (Moses 5:4–5).

Through prayers we draw nigh to the only person powerful enough to overcome the disordering influence of Satan. "Verily, verily, I say unto you, ye must watch and pray always, lest ye be tempted by the devil, and ye be led away captive by him. And as I have prayed among you even so shall ye pray in my church, among my people who do repent and are baptized in my name. Behold I am the light; I have set an example for you" (3 Nephi 18:15–16).

Through prayer we remind ourselves of our duties to overcome disorder and we receive guidance on how to do it. A favorite hymn describes the ordering consequences of prayer:

Sweet hour of prayer! Sweet hour of prayer!
That calls me from a world of care.
And bids me at my Father's throne
Make all my wants and wishes known.
In seasons of distress and grief
My soul has often found relief
And oft escaped the tempter's snare
By thy return, sweet hour of prayer!
And oft escaped the tempter's snare
By thy return, sweet hour of prayer![4]

Related to the need for prayer is the need for the ordering that occurs in ordinances that put into effect promises between man and God. The ordinances, an important means of coming to Christ, connect us to each other and the Savior by putting into effect covenants. The covenants and coming to Christ bring about order. Indeed, the root of the word *order* is "ord" and is used in the word *ordinance*—the process of putting into effect promises between man and God. Thus, ordinances bring order to the Church and our lives by establishing expectations and obligations.

One important ordinance is the ordination of worthy males to the priesthood. To ordain to the priesthood means to bring order by conferring on worthy males the power and authority to act for God in the way the Lord has commanded. When priesthood quorums and individuals carry out their specific responsibilities, there is order in the Church.

9. Work

Perhaps one of the most important messages the Lord gave Adam and Eve was to work hard. "And it came to pass that after I, the Lord God, had driven them out, that Adam began to till the earth, and to have dominion over all the beasts of the field, and to eat his bread by the sweat of his brow, as I the Lord had commanded him. And Eve, also, his wife, did labor with him" (Moses 5:1).

God commanded perspiration-producing work—physical, mental, and emotional. Nothing of any significance was achieved without work. The joy of the laborer cannot be experienced without work. The work the Lord required of Adam and Eve was creative-organizing work. "Dress this Garden, take care of it. Beautify it." Weeds are plants growing out of place and should be removed. Clothes and things out of place are clutter and should be picked up. You can't tell what your capacities are unless you accept responsibilities to work.

President Thomas S. Monson one time described the need for hard work. "Work will win when wishy-washy wishing won't. Should you be discouraged, look back carefully and honestly and you will find that your work has not been done with all your might. Victory is bound to come to him who gives all of himself to the cause he represents when there [is] truth in the cause. There is no place for procrastination, defined by Edward Young two centuries ago as 'the thief of time.'"[5]

There is a special blessing reserved for families (and Church organizations) that learn how to work together. Work has a powerful organizing capacity in ways similar to selecting goals. When we have work to do, we are placing order above disorder. While consuming is necessary and also pleasant, it is work that creates. Working with friends and family for a common cause also builds at-one-ment. Working together is a much different experience than consuming for individual pleasure, because work connects us. No family or auxiliary will be entirely successful without focusing a significant portion of its efforts on work and service.

One more reason for work and service is that they rescue us from the tugging tendencies of the natural world that would carry us downstream to places below and beneath what we deserve. Laman and Lemuel asked Nephi to interpret the river which their father Lehi saw in vision. Nephi responded, "The water which my father saw was filthiness; and so much was his mind swallowed up in other things that he beheld not the filthiness of the water" (1 Nephi 15:27).

To work hard is not enough, though. We must work toward results. I'm not sure that we should simply call "energy-demanding exertions" work. To give proper order to our efforts, they must be directed toward an increase. Adam and Eve were commanded to multiply and replenish the earth. The most limited interpretation of this instruction means to multiply their children, and surely this was the main message. But we might increase this meaning to include multiplying your talents, your service, the converts you have helped, and the people you have served.

Finally, there is one thing to learn about how to organize from the Creation. On the seventh day when the Creation was completed, the Lord rested. One of our mistakes is that we too often rest before we finish our work, and because we make this unfortunate mix, we never complete our tasks.

10. Reflect and Report

After Adam and Eve disobeyed the Lord and partook of the fruit of the tree of knowledge of good and evil, the Lord returned and asked them to report. In the process of reporting, several important acts of ordering occurred. First, Adam and Eve compared where they were with where they needed to be.

Someone once said that it took the children of Israel forty years of wandering in the wilderness to reach Canaan because they wouldn't stop and ask for directions. Reporting directs us to examine where we are on the map. Then, depending on our progress, reporting our efforts can direct us to course corrections. The process also requires that we accept responsibility for who we have become, which is essential in the repentance process. Lastly, reporting leads us to new resolves, so we renew our covenants and commitments to keep the commandments.

The sacrament service is one of our special times to reflect and report, to renew our covenants, report our progress, acknowledge our imperfections, resolve to make any amends and renew our efforts to achieve our goals.

ଓ ଞ

Brother and Sister Williams sat nervously in front of Bishop Blunt. After offering a brief prayer, Bishop Blunt came straight to the point. "Brother and Sister Williams, I want you to know that your home teachers and visiting teachers love and care for you and your family." Then laying his glasses on his desk, he looked at them kindly, but with a certain resolve to not minimize the need for their interview. "Frankly, your home is a disorganized mess that is an embarrassment to your children and friends. You represent the Church to your neighbors…and, because of your lack of organization, it leaves them with a less than favorable image of you and the church you represent."

Brother Williams could feel his temper rising, but his wife's firm hand on his arm calmed him. "Fortunately," the bishop continued, "there is a solution…a way to create order and beauty out of chaos. Would you make a list as I review the creative steps the Lord followed during the Creation?"

"One…meet with your family and set a goal for making your home a place of beauty. Then you must make a plan for achieving your goal. A goal without a plan is a wistful dream. So plan.

"Two…your plan must designate a place for every thing. Then each member of the family must agree to put everything that belongs to them in its place. 'Everything with a place and everything in its place' must become your motto.

"Three…the heart of the plan must require that *like* things belong together and are separated from those things from which they differ. Cars belong in the garage. Toys belong in the toy box when not in use. Dirty dishes and couches are not alike and must be separated…dirty dishes in the dishwasher and people on the couches.

"Four…plan to do the most important things first. The most important things are those that lead you to success…a house of beauty and order. Television programs must not take priority over homework and doing household duties. Attending sporting events and recreational activities must not take priority over painting one's house and making needed repairs…such as fixing doors that do not open and close, toilets that do not flush, and water faucets that do not shut off."

Then the bishop, raising his voice for emphasis, demanded,

"Five…you must call things by their right names. Much of what passes on TV is not suitable entertainment for families. Call it what it *is*…worldly sensations designed to desensitize our spirits. Call it and the music that goes with it by their right names… *trash*.

"Six…Brother and Sister Williams," Bishop Blunt hesitated, "…one of the main reasons that you lead such disorganized lives is that you are not working together. An ordered home requires that you share the same vision and commit yourselves to working together. You must attend first to your marriage. Then you will be successful in your dealings with others."

The bishop continued reassuringly,

"Seven…there are homemaking skills just like there are skills for doing other jobs. Sister Williams, your visiting teachers have volunteered to spend next Saturday helping you organize your home…beginning with your kitchen. Brother Williams, your home teachers have agreed to help you organize your garage. Will you accept their training?" Brother and Sister Williams nodded their assent. "They will also bring a large trailer to haul away the accumulated clutter that in truth has no place and is a threat to an organized home," continued the bishop.

"Eight…the physical condition of our homes often mirrors the spiritual climate in our homes. Begin a tradition of daily family prayers and scripture study. Religiously observe family home evenings. Kindle the fire of your own testimonies. Then notice how improving the spiritual climate of your home leads naturally to improving the physical condition in your home.

"Nine…what would be helpful for you and your family would be to finish what you've started before resting and starting a new project." Patiently, Bishop Blunt asked, "Do you remember when, during the Creation, the Lord rested?" Then Bishop Blunt answered his own question. "After the work was done."

Brother Williams felt convicted. His car restoration, his garage cleaning project, his rock garden, and painting his house were all unfinished projects—none of which had a completion date. Sister Williams felt the same. Cleaning the kitchen, the bathrooms, and organizing the storage room were all projects that were repeatedly started, but never finished.

Finally, the bishop reminded the Williams of the great love he and the ward members felt for them. Bishop Blunt told Brother and Sister Williams that they were great resources in the ward— always willing to help and to give comfort to those in need.

"Finally…ten…can we meet in three weeks at your house to review your progress?"

They agreed and the bishop closed their meeting with a prayer, asking for the Lord's help in their efforts to create a house of order and beauty. And as Brother and Sister Williams left the bishop's office, Brother Williams put his arm around his wife's shoulders and for the first time in a long time, they had hope.

Conclusions

God organized the world. Then He commanded that Adam and Eve care for and beautify His Creation. The commandment has not been rescinded or revoked. While we may not be responsible for the Garden of Eden, we each have some portion of God's Creation to care for. The musician is responsible for creating order and beauty out of sounds. The author is responsible for creating order and beauty out of the written word. Families have the responsibility for creating beautiful homes and family relations. As we mature in our creative responsibilities, we may become more aware of the connections between beauty and harmonious relationships. A home filled with beautiful paintings and music that calms the soul all contribute to the at-one-ment in the home. As we magnify our stewardships, we become co-creators and more like God whom we strive to follow.

NOTES

1. *Teachings of the Prophet Joseph Smith,* sel. Joseph Fielding Smith, (1976), 350–51.

2. Gerald N. Lund. "Fire of the Covenant," Dawn Anderson, Dlora Dalton, and Susette Green, eds., *Every Good Thing: Talks from the 1997 BYU Women's Conference,* 281.

3. *The Collins English Dictionary, 21st Century Edition,* (2000).

4. "Sweet Hour of Prayer," *Hymns of The Church of Jesus Christ of Latter-day Saints*, no. 142.

5. Thomas S. Monson, *Be Your Best Self,* (1979), 117.

Chapter Ten

LEARNING BY STUDY AND FAITH

Understandest thou what thou readest?
And he [the Ethiopian] said, How can I,
except some man should guide me?

—Acts 8:30–31

CR ⁊⊃

Amy and John sat in the back of their daughter Samantha's first grade classroom with John's parents. Samantha turned around in her desk near the front of the class to confirm
her support group's presence. Amy waved and smiled. Samantha
smiled and waved back and then looked at her teacher, confidently.
Miss Plum addressed the class. "Today we are pleased to have
with us Samantha's parents and one set of her grandparents." Miss
Plum continued. "Samantha's grandparents will soon be leaving
for Spain where they will live for three years, presiding over a
mission for their church. To help prepare them for their assignment
and to help us learn about Spain, Samantha has prepared a special
show and tell this morning."

Samantha stood and faced the class. Then she ***explained,*** "My
grandparents are going to live in Spain, and in Spain they have
bull fights." Continuing, Samantha reached into her plastic sack
and pulled out a bull-fighter's hat and a red cape. Placing the hat
on her head and holding the cape to her side, she continued her
explanation. "In Spain, they have a bull and a bull fighter. The

bull fighter is called a matador, and in a place with a big fence the matador holds out his cape and waves it at the bull." Then Samantha **demonstrated** the proper matador stance and waved her cape. "Then the bull gets mad and runs into the cape and everybody yells 'Ole!'" Then she invited her friend Beth to pretend to be a bull and to hold her hands on her head so they looked like horns. Beth then sprinted through the cape, and the class in unison yelled "Ole!"

"Okay," Samantha continued. "Now you all get to **practice** being bulls and matadors." Samantha then passed out red caps that Amy had prepared out of cotton cloth the night before. For a few minutes chaos reigned as the future matadors practiced deftly moving to the side to avoid charging bulls. Then, with no small effort, Miss Plum called the class back to order and thanked Samantha for her show and tell and **encouraged** the class, "You were great bull fighters and hopefully sometime in the future you will all visit Spain. Now for the next few minutes we are going to learn a little more about Spain and its traditions. Can anyone tell me which great explorer sailed from Spain and discovered the Americas?"

Some time later during their missionary service, Samantha's grandparents learned about the teaching model that included four steps—explain, demonstrate, practice, and encourage and evaluate. Samantha's grandparents found that as the missionaries used this model, their teaching improved, and investigators better understood their messages. Then Samantha's grandparents remembered that they had already been introduced to the teaching model—in a first-grade classroom—by their granddaughter Samantha who had never heard of such a model, but instinctively knew how to apply it.

The Teaching Model

We all sense at-one-ment or separation through our minds, hearts, hands, and feet. We also learn the ways of at-one-ment through these same senses. While we all possess these four senses of at-one-ment, we possess them in different levels of development. Indeed, our personalities may reflect our preference for learning through one or more of these senses. Some learn best with their minds, others with their hearts, and still others with their hands or feet. Yet, each of our four senses provides unique information, and complete learning requires that they all be educated.

A popular teaching model engages and informs all four senses.[1] The model can be applied to both teachers and students and is described graphically below.

Stage 1. Explain to the mind.

Stage 2. Demonstrate to the hands.

Stage 3. Practice with the feet.

Stage 4. Evaluate and provide feedback that gives direction and encourages the heart.

Of course, the order of the stages may be altered and any one stage may be repeated depending on the needs of the students.

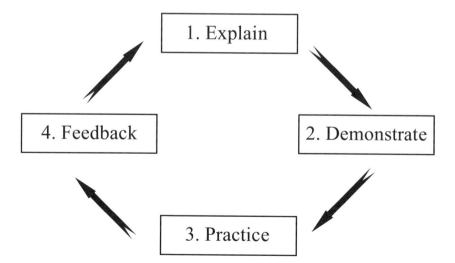

Successful teachers educate all four of our senses. Truly educated men and women understand with their minds, envision possibilities for good with their hands, care deeply in their hearts about using their knowledge to bless others, and act on their possibilities to do good with their feet.

The world has known geniuses who, inspired by a dark power, gained knowledge, but failed to apply it to bless others. Such was the case of German rocket scientists in World War II who invented the V-class rockets to bomb the people and cities of Europe. The world has also known good men who desired to bless others, but because of a lack of knowledge, did great damage. Such was the case of the physicians who "bled" President George Washington believing they were administering aid, but in the end cost him his life. A truly educated person not only knows, but envisions, cares, and does the right thing.

President Gordon B. Hinckley taught that we should be educated both mentally and spiritually, and the latter can only occur when we are touched by the Holy Ghost. "There is concern that some people in the Church have mental, but not spiritual conversion. The gospel appeals to them, but real conversion is when they feel something in their hearts and not just in their minds. There is mental assent, but not spiritual conviction. They must be touched by the power of the Holy Ghost that creates in them a spiritual experience. Then the power and deep conversion of the Spirit confirms to them what they have agreed to in their minds. This testimony of the heart and not just the head, will carry them through every storm of adversity."[2]

In what follows we explore the learning and teaching process that employs our four senses of at-one-ment. We then emphasize that the most effective teaching and learning requires the at-one-ment of the teacher and student—and both with the Holy Ghost. Progress has been impeded and often reversed when this at-one-ment between teacher and students and the Spirit was lacking. Finally, the most effective teaching and learning employs the Spirit that enlightens our minds, gladdens our hearts, expands our visions, and empowers our service.

The Teaching Model and Teachers

The first requirement to be a great teacher is to be a great student, having willingly employed all of one's senses in learning the lessons to be taught. Great teachers study their lessons out in their minds. They live what they have learned, demonstrating the lessons they intend to teach in their daily walk. They feel deeply about the subjects they intend to teach and care for their students. Then, great teachers commit themselves and their students to act, to practice, and to experience the lessons they need to learn.

Great teachers who have educated their senses of at-one-ment before they teach are like persons standing on higher ground, who can see farther than others and wish to share their view with their friends. As a result of their preparation, great teachers "teach with power and authority" (Mosiah 18:26). Isaac Newton, a famous scientist and mathematician, one time wrote his friend, Robert Hooke, a letter in which he acknowledged his dependence on great teachers. "If I have seen farther than others, it is because I was standing on the shoulders of giants."

Stage 1

In the first stage of the teaching model, the teacher awakens the minds of the students by explaining the concepts to be learned. The teacher may awaken the students' minds by connecting questions and answers, choices and their consequences, and by distinguishing between things that are similar from those that are distinct. The teacher may also help the student to recognize sequences in which some things must come before others and to identify synergy from right combinations and friction from wrong ones.

Stage 2

In the second stage of the teaching model, the teacher appeals to the visual senses of the students. In this stage of the model, the teacher demonstrates the lesson so the students can see what is to be done and what is to be learned. This step involves creating a vision of the desired outcome—a wise application of what has been explained. Without a vision, the students are often uninterested. Often this visual portion of the lesson can be achieved by relating a personal experience or an experience of others. Pictures and other illustrations may be used as well.

When the lesson involves a virtue to be learned, the teacher best illustrates the lesson by consistently living what they teach. Elder Paul Dunn quoted Ralph Waldo Emerson who said, "What you do thunders so loudly in my ears I cannot hear what you say." Then Elder Dunn added, "Parents can tell, but never teach until they practice what they preach."[3]

Stage 3

In the third stage of the teaching model, the teacher commits the student to practice—a doing activity that educates one's feet. In this stage of the model, the teacher invites the learner to practice until the action can be performed almost independently of the other senses. For example, most accomplished pianists do not communicate detailed instruction to their hands to play the piano, but have over time trained their hands to act on their own.

Elder Loren C. Dunn wrote about his father who recognized the importance of having opportunities for his sons to practice. He wrote that growing up in a small community, his father saw the need for him and his brother to practice farm work. So his father put him and his brother to work on a small farm while he, their father, ran the local newspaper. Then Elder Dunn reported, "Our small farm was surrounded by other farms, and one of the farmers went in to see my father one day to tell him the things he thought we were doing wrong. My father listened to him carefully and then said, 'Jim, you don't understand. You see, I'm raising boys and not cows.'"[4]

Stage 4

Finally, in the fourth stage of the teaching model, the teacher provides feedback to the students. The teacher's feedback recognizes the students' efforts already extended and encourages them to try to do what has not yet been achieved. In this stage of the learning process, the teacher offers his or her students suggestions for improvement and congratulates them on their progress. This stage of the model, of course, can only be effective if the teacher genuinely cares about his or her students. So the teacher expresses love and caring. The desired outcome of this stage of the learning process is to animate the hearts of the learners so that they continue to keep trying.

Playing the Piano

Perhaps the teaching model can be better understood with an example. Consider how the model can be applied to teachers helping their students learn to play the piano. The teacher begins by explaining the basic theory of music and the connection between the length of resonating wires and their representation written on sheets of music. Next, the teacher demonstrates how the coordinated movements of one hand on the piano with the notes written on a sheet of music can produce a sound of harmony to both one's body and spirit. Then the teacher assigns the student to practice and begin the training in which the mind and heart command the body to realize the vision of musical possibilities. Later, after the student has made some progress in his or her practice, the teacher encourages, corrects, and directs future learning efforts.

The Teaching Model and the Student

Stage 1

In the first stage of the teaching model, the student is attentive and recognizes the competence of the teacher. We might call this requirement, having faith in one's teacher. Then, the student opens his mind to understanding and studies the lesson that has been explained to him. The student brings to this phase of the model questions and concerns that motivate him or her to look for answers. Is the lesson logical? Is it believable? Does it have application to me? Is it important?

Stage 2

In the second step of the model, the student must develop a vision of how the lesson can be learned and applied. He must not only understand the material in his mind, but he or she must see it as well.

An example that illustrates the importance of a vision in the learning process occurred in the life of Philo T. Farnsworth, the inventor of modern electronic television. The moment of inspiration came while he was breaking up soil with his uncle's horse-drawn harrow, row by row. He imagined how an electron beam could scan images the same way, line by line, just as you read a book, row by row or line by line. And so from this vision a new information revolution began.[5]

Stage 3

The third step of the model employs the feet. It requires that the student practice. Understanding with the mind and seeing with one's hands can never provide all of the information required for understanding. The Lord explained the connection between learning and doing in a revelation to Joseph Smith in which the Lord declared, "He that keepeth [my] commandments receiveth truth and light, until he is glorified in truth and knoweth all things" (D&C 93:28).

President Heber J. Grant demonstrated the importance of practice in the learning process. He practiced singing, penmanship, and baseball until he became proficient in each—but at the cost of persistent practice. Writing about the practice required to become proficient in baseball, President Grant wrote, "Often my arm would ache so that I could scarcely go to sleep at night, but I kept on practicing and finally succeeded in getting into the second nine [players] of our club. Subsequently, I joined a better club and eventually played with the nine that won the championship in California, Colorado, and Wyoming, and thus made good my promise to myself and retired from the baseball arena."[6]

Stage 4

In the fourth stage, the student must feel encouraged, confident in his or her success, and a desire to succeed in mastering the lesson. When the student has acquired this change of heart, learning no longer becomes a burden, but a noble quest.

An early Apostle, Parley P. Pratt, described the condition of his heart that led to his gaining a testimony of the Book of Mormon. "I opened [the Book of Mormon] with eagerness, and read its title page. I then read the testimony of several witnesses in relation to the manner of its being found and translated. After this I commenced its contents by course. I read all day; eating was a burden, I had no desire for food; sleep was a burden when the night came, for I preferred reading to sleep.... As I read, the spirit of the Lord was upon me, and I knew and comprehended that the book was true, as plainly and manifestly as a man comprehends and knows that he exists."[7]

At-one-ment of Teachers and Students

Effective application of the teaching model requires at-one-ment of the student and the teacher. This at-one-ment of the teacher and the student requires that at least four things are present in them both.

First, the teacher must know his lessons. Second, the teacher must be able to create a visual image of his lesson, often by exemplifying them in his life. Third, the teacher must allow the student to practice, to experience the lessons to be learned. Fourth, the teacher must love the students and care deeply about the subject to be taught.

Students on the other hand, must first trust their teacher and have confidence in his or her ability to pass on the desired skill. Second, the student must envision the end, what is he or she to achieve. Third, the student must practice and apply the lessons to be learned. Finally, the student must have the desire to learn and confidence that the desired end can be achieved.

Creating At-one-ment by Adapting the Lesson to the Students

Great teachers are able to create at-one-ment with their students who are different from themselves by adapting their message to their students. One way we adapt our teaching to the senses of our students is through the kinds of questions that we ask. Questions invite those being taught to make a connection. Questions directed to the *mind* of persons being taught ask them to make connections between our message and their understanding, using reasoned or logical connections. For example, we might ask, "Do you think that God has the power to call and communicate to a prophet today as He did in times past?"

Questions directed to the *heart* of persons being taught ask them to make connections between our message and their feelings.

Like, "How does it make you feel to know that God is your loving Heavenly Father?"

Questions directed to the visual (*hands*) nature of persons being taught ask them to see or visualize a connection between our message and their seeing—the Savior used parables and metaphors to help his audiences connect to his message. We might ask, "Can you see or imagine the similarities between a growing seed and your testimony of our message?"

Finally, questions directed to the doing (*feet*) side of our natures of persons being taught ask them to connect to our message by doing or acting. For instance, "After you have read about the importance of baptism in the Book of Mormon, will you pray and ask God whether you should be baptized, and when?"

In addition, if a learner has the tendency to learn with his mind, then the teacher will emphasize reason and logic. If the learner has the tendency to learn visually through his hands, then the teacher will emphasize visual aids and mental images. If the learner has the tendency to learn with his heart, the wise teacher will express feelings. Finally, for those that learn with their feet, the wise teacher will provide opportunities for action during the lesson.

Finally, Paul demonstrated the need to adapt his message to the learning capacity of his hearers when he taught, "For though I be free from all men, yet have I made myself servant unto all, that I might gain the more. And unto the Jews I became as a Jew, that I might gain the Jews; to them that are under the law, as under the law, that I might gain them that are under the law; To them that are without law, as without law, (being not without law to God, but under the law to Christ,) that I might gain them that are without law. To the weak became I as weak, that I might gain the weak: I am made all things to all men, that I might by all means save some" (1 Corinthians 9:19–22).

Failed Lessons

The history of the world is littered by unwilling students and unprepared teachers whose failures to teach and learn have led to human sufferings and missed opportunities. Consider the unsuccessful application of the teaching model to Laman and Lemuel and the separation and wars that followed.

Lehi was a master teacher. He had learned his material from angels and revelations from God. He demonstrated his lessons in his daily walk. He committed his family over and over again to keep the commandments. He loved his family. Yet, Laman and Lemuel failed to learn. They failed to learn first of all because they lacked confidence in Lehi their father, primarily because their hearts were focused on other things. They "did murmur in many things against their father, because he was a visionary man, and had led them out of the land of Jerusalem, to leave the land of their inheritance, and their gold, and their silver, and their precious things, to perish in the wilderness. And this they said he had done because of the foolish imaginations of his heart" (1 Nephi 2:11).

These slow-to-learn students, Laman and Lemuel, also failed to learn because they refused to practice what they had been taught, leading Lehi to lament, "O [Lemuel] that thou mightest be like unto this valley, firm and steadfast, and immovable in keeping the commandments of the Lord!" (1 Nephi 2:10). They also failed to learn because they were unwilling to study their lessons. These difficult students complained, "Behold, we cannot understand the words which our father hath spoken concerning the natural branches of the olive-tree, and also concerning the Gentiles" (1 Nephi 15:7). To which Nephi asked, "Have ye inquired of the Lord?" (1 Nephi 15:8). They answered, "We have not; for the Lord maketh no such thing known unto us" (1 Nephi 15:9).

Sometimes learning fails to occur because of unwilling students, as in the case of Laman and Lemuel. On other occasions, learning may fail to occur because of wicked and poorly prepared teachers, as in the case of the priests of wicked King Noah.

The prophet Abinadi chastised the priests of King Noah whose failure to teach the people led them to apostasy. "Wo be unto you for perverting the ways of the Lord! For if ye understand these things ye have not taught them; therefore, ye have perverted the ways of the Lord" (Mosiah 12:26). Their failure to teach the ways of at-one-ment was because they did not desire to learn the ways of the Lord. They had not "applied [their] hearts to understanding; therefore, [they had] not been wise" (Mosiah 12:27). Finally, even though they taught the Law of Moses to the people, they failed to demonstrate its application in their lives. Therefore Abinadi condemned them. "If ye teach the Law of Moses why do ye not keep it?" (Mosiah 12:29). The consequence of the terrible teaching of King Noah's priests, as it always is, was apostasy, separations, and destruction.

The One Master Teacher

Our Savior, the Master Teacher, appealed to all four senses of at-one-ment of His students. John records how He appealed to the *minds* of His students. "Now about the midst of the feast Jesus went up into the temple, and taught. And the Jews marvelled, saying, How knoweth this man letters, having never learned?" (John 7:14–15). Recognizing He had the words of eternal life, Nicodemus addressed him as "a teacher come from God: for no man can do these miracles that thou doest, except God be with him" (John 3:2).

Jesus also taught the *hearts* of His disciples because He loved them. For example, He demonstrated His love to His friends and disciples Mary and Martha at the death of their brother Lazarus. "Then when Mary was come where Jesus was, and saw him, she fell down at his feet, saying unto him, Lord, if thou hadst been here, my brother had not died. When Jesus therefore saw her weeping, and the Jews also weeping which came with her, He groaned in the spirit, and was troubled, and said, Where have ye laid him? They said unto him, Lord, come and see. Jesus wept. Then said the Jews, Behold how he loved him!" (John 11:32–36).

Jesus frequently created visual images for His disciples by using parables to appeal to their *hands*. His images were metaphors that equated His followers to a light on a hill, His missionaries to a sower of seeds and fishers of men, and hypocrites to whited sepulchres. He compared one's efforts to find the gospel to a person seeking a "pearl of great price." He taught the importance of a lost soul by comparing her to a lost lamb that the good shepherd searches in the wilderness to find and then rejoices when the lost is found.

More importantly, Christ lived His lessons. When He taught that no greater love has one man for another than to lay down his life, He lived His lessons and offered Himself a sacrifice for sin to save all of us whom He loves.

Finally, the Savior committed His disciples to live and practice the lessons He taught them, and to do the things they had seen Him do. He healed the leper, He changed water into wine, He cleansed the temple twice, and He called apostles and organized His Church. He taught His gospel and carried His cross—literally and symbolically—carrying our crosses as well. Then our Savior counseled His disciples, "For the works which ye have seen me do that shall ye also do; for that which ye have seen me do even that shall ye do" (3 Nephi 27:21). And in the Old World He commanded His disciples, "Go ye into all the world, and preach the gospel to every creature" (Mark 16:15). These were commitments to do, to put one's *feet* on the path the Savior had walked.

Revelation and Learning

There is an unalterable fact in the world of teaching and learning. Our progress requires that we teach and learn what at one time no one knew. This fact leads us to important questions such as, who opened Philo T. Farnsworth's mind to envision the possibility of modern television? Who taught Isaac Newton calculus? Who inspired Edison to invent the telephone, the electric light, and many other modern miracles? No teachers that we know were available to pass on these breakthroughs in knowledge whose widespread applications have changed the world.

There is one information source that knew and could communicate to the minds of these willing students, the Light of Christ and the Holy Ghost. For example, the Lord commands His saints to "preach my gospel by the Spirit, even the Comforter which was sent forth to teach the truth" (D&C 50:14).

However, the Light of Christ and the Holy Ghost can only teach when there is an at-one-ment of the student and the teacher. The Lord revealed that those sent to preach the gospel must do so by the Spirit of Truth (see D&C 50:17). Furthermore, those that receive the preaching must also receive it by the Spirit of Truth, and if it is received any other way, it is not of God (see D&C 50:19–20). Of course, revelations may come from sources other than from the Holy Ghost. The difference between the revelations sent by the Holy Ghost and by the forces of darkness is that which comes of God will edify, build up, elevate, and enliven. "That which doth not edify is not of God, and is darkness. That which is of God is light; and He that receiveth light, and continueth in God, receiveth more light; and that light groweth brighter and brighter until the perfect day" (D&C 50:23–24).

The teaching capacity of the Holy Ghost described in the scriptures includes the following:

1. The Holy Ghost will reveal truth to our minds and to our hearts (see D&C 8:2) and bring to our remembrance former lessons of the Spirit (see John 14:26).

2. The Holy Ghost will animate our hearts with joy, peace, and hope (see Romans 15:13).

3. The Holy Ghost teaches beyond the wisdom of man, leading us to expand our understanding of things of the Spirit (see 1 Corinthians 2:12–13).

4. Finally, it is through the Holy Ghost that those who will listen may know of the things they are to do (see 2 Nephi 32:5).

Of course, the teachings of the Holy Ghost are available only to those who desire to be taught, as was Nephi who wrote, "I, Nephi, was desirous also that I might see, and hear, and know of these things, [including the knowledge of the Messiah who should come] by the power of the Holy Ghost, which is the gift of God unto all those who diligently seek him, as well in times of old as in the time that he should manifest himself unto the children of men" (1 Nephi 10:17).

Conclusions

Great teachers who enjoy at-one-ment with their students enlighten minds, open visions, provide opportunities to practice, and then gladden hearts. To the *heart* of their students, great teachers express love. To the *mind* of their students they share understanding. To the *hands* of their students, they provide an example to follow. To the *feet* of their students, they work side by side.

Yet great teachers teach one other thing. They help their students realize the difference and relative importance of spiritual versus secular knowledge. The knowledge revealed to Philo T. Farnsworth has brought untold blessings to the world when it has been used wisely. But it has not saved a single soul. Only in Christ do we have hope for salvation.

President Spencer W. Kimball taught that "we must recognize that secular knowledge alone can never save a soul nor open the celestial kingdom to anyone.... Yet secular knowledge can be most helpful to the children of our Father in Heaven who, having placed first things first, have found and are living those truths which lead one to eternal life."[8]

Since God is the author of all truth, those who learn best learn through the Spirit. Of course, like grace, learning new truths requires that we do all that we can to prepare to receive revelation. Fortunately, every man is born into this world with the Spirit of Christ to reveal to him the difference between good and evil (see Moroni 7:16).

A testimony is a special kind of knowledge of God and of the goodness and the truthfulness of His plan of happiness. Moroni explains that this special knowledge can only be learned when the student is aided by the Holy Ghost. "And when ye shall receive these things, I would exhort you that ye would ask God, the Eternal Father, in the name of Christ, if these things are not true; and if ye shall ask with a sincere heart, with real intent, having faith in Christ, he will manifest the truth of it unto you, by the power of the Holy Ghost. And by the power of the Holy Ghost ye may know the truth of all things" (Moroni 10:4–5).

NOTES

1. http://www.pacwcbt.pitt.edu/curriculum

2. Quoted by Elder Gerald N. Lund, BYU-Idaho Devotional, March 25, 2003.

3. Paul H. Dunn, "Parents, Teach Your Children," *Ensign,* May 1974, 14.

4. Loren C. Dunn, "Our Precious Families," *Ensign,* November 1974, 9.

5. Vince Horiuchi, "Mormon Farm Boy: Inventor of Television" *Salt Lake Tribune,* March 2000, 20.

6. Bryant S. Hinckley, *Heber J. Grant*, (1951), 37–38.

7. *Autobiography of Parley P. Pratt,* ed. Parley P. Pratt Jr., (1938), 36–37.

8. Spencer W. Kimball, "'Seek Learning, Even by Study and Also by Faith'," *Ensign*, September 1983, 3.

Epilogue

ATONEMENT AND AT-ONE-MENT

That they all may be one; as thou, Father, art in me,
and I in thee, that they also may be one in us:
that the world may believe that thou hast sent me
—John 17:21

ଓଃ ଋ

After Sunday School, the ward members reassembled for sacrament meeting. And after the preliminaries, Amy stood to lead the congregation in singing the sacrament hymn, "God our Father, Hear Us Pray." The priests were still breaking the bread at the sacrament table when the song ended so Amy invited the members to hum the melody of the hymn. Later that evening, she recorded in her journal what happened next:

> *As I looked out over the congregation, every member seemed to be humming and reflecting on the message of the hymn and the beauty and harmony of the song filled the chapel. I was overcome with emotion as I listened to the beauty of the sound and felt the presence of the Holy Spirit. I looked at John and caught his eye and could tell he was feeling what I was feeling. It was and is a powerful testimony to me that as we unite in singing the hymns, we become one because we invite the presence of the Holy Spirit. My heart still fills with emotion remembering the beauty of that moment. This is a testimony to me of the importance and opportunity to actively unite in worshiping through the hymns. I truly felt the Holy Spirit's presence as we hummed the melody of the sacrament hymn.*

The Atonement of Jesus Christ and At-one-ment

Because of the Atonement of Jesus Christ, we and all man-kind may be saved—brought to at-one-ment. This possibility of at-one-ment means that we can become persons of integrity, entirely converted and complete in our collection of Christlike virtues. It means that we can cleave to each other with our hearts, minds, hands, and feet and live in a Zion—and as a Zion people (see D&C 88:40). Finally, it means that after having done all that we can and should do to become converted and to become a Zion people, we can qualify for eternal life, to live with and be like our Father in Heaven and Jesus Christ whom He sent to redeem us. And all of these at-one-ments are possible because of and through the power of Christ's Atonement (see Ether 3: 14).

The Perfect Example of At-one-ment

The Father and the Son are the perfect example of at-one-ment. Furthermore, the Savior taught His disciples that they should strive for the at-one-ment that exists between Him and His Father. He prayed, "That they all may be one; as thou, Father, *art* in me, and I in thee" (John 17:21).

Describing the at-one-ment of the Godhead, President Gordon B. Hinckley stated, "They [the members of the Godhead] are distinct beings, but They are one in purpose and effort. They are united as one in bringing to pass the grand, divine plan for the salvation and exaltation of the children of God."[1] And on a different occasion, President Hinckley taught, "It is that perfect unity between the Father, the Son, and the Holy Ghost that binds these three into the oneness of the divine Godhead."[2] So in our efforts to achieve at-one-ment, we look to the example set by the Father and the Son to guide our own efforts.

We marvel at the depth of their divine unity when we read the Savior's words offering His total Being to complete the Father's plan and to obey His will. "I seek not mine own will, but the will of the Father which hath sent me" (John 5:30) and "Father, thy will be done, and the glory be thine forever" (Moses 4:2).

We are inspired by the Savior's single-minded commitment to do the will of His Father, even at an early age when He gently reminded Mary and Joseph of His divine duty. "And he said unto them, How is it that ye sought me? Wist ye not that I must be about my Father's business?" (Luke 2:49).

We are strengthened in our vision for at-one-ment when we imagine the Savior explaining to His disciples, "Verily, verily, I say unto you, The Son can do nothing of himself, but what he seeth the Father do; for what things soever he doeth, these also doeth the Son likewise. For the Father loveth the Son, and sheweth him all things that himself doeth; and he will shew him greater works than these, that ye may marvel" (John 5:19–20).

We are encouraged to keep trying for at-one-ment when we understand that, like the Savior, we are not alone when tested and tried. "Then said Jesus unto them, When ye have lifted up the Son of man, then shall ye know that I am he, and that I do nothing of myself; but as my Father hath taught me, . . . And he that sent me is with me: the Father hath not left me alone; for I do always those things that please him" (John 8:28–29).

We stand all amazed at the Savior's commitment to do the will of His Father when in the moment of His supreme opportunity and sorrow, He submitted Himself to the will of the Father, saying, "Father, if thou be willing, remove this cup from me: nevertheless not my will, but thine, be done" (Luke 22:42). With Christ's act of Atonement and His at-one-ment with the Father, He now pleads for us and our at-one-ment having gained the victory over death and having power to make intercession for us before the Father (see Mosiah 15:7–8).

And we are fortified to act courageously to defend what is sacred as we simulate in our souls the Savior's response to those who stained His Father's house. "And when he had made a scourge of small cords, he drove them all out of the temple, and the sheep, and the oxen: and poured out the changers' money, and overthrew the tables; And said unto them that sold doves, Take these things hence; make not my Father's house an house of merchandise" (John 2:15–16).

And after having gained all and in every way having become perfect like His Father, the Savior commands His disciples everywhere to seek for the same. "Therefore, I would that ye should be perfect even as I, or your Father who is in heaven is perfect" (3 Nephi 12:48).

The Savior's path to perfection led Him to do and become all that His Father had done and become. He taught Philip, "Have I been so long time with you, and yet hast thou not known me, Philip? He that hath seen me hath seen the Father; and how sayest thou then, Shew us the Father?" (John 14:9).

Likewise our quest for at-one-ment is nothing more or less than to become like God and to be glorified by the same glory by which He was glorified. The Savior promised, "And the glory which thou gavest me I have given them; that they may be one, even as we are one" (John 17:22).

As we learn about the perfect at-one-ment that exists between the Father and the Son, our attention is drawn to one quality of their unity that shines above all the rest. Of course, the Son did the things He saw His Father do. Of course the doctrine He taught was not His, but His Father's. Of course, the plan of salvation of which His Atonement was the integral part, was His Father's. But the depth of Their at-one-ment can only be measured by Their infinite love for each other.

The Father emblazoned in our scriptures His consummate love for His son in His prologue to His Son's ministry. "And Jesus, when he was baptized, went up straightway out of the water: and, lo, the heavens were opened unto him, and he saw the Spirit of God descending like a dove, and lighting upon him: and lo a voice from heaven, saying, This is my beloved Son, in whom I am well pleased" (Matthew 3:16–17). Jesus filled with His Father's love offered the same to His disciples. "As the Father hath loved me, so have I loved you: continue ye in my love" (John 15:9).

Then in the New World the Father speaking from the heavens declared the infinite expanse of His love for His Son. "Behold my Beloved Son, in whom I am well pleased, in whom I have glorified my name—hear ye him" (3 Nephi 11:6–7).

The Atonement and Our At-one-ment

In addition to His suffering endured, His love displayed, and His power manifest in the Garden of Gethsemane, on the cross, and at the tomb of Arimathaea, the Atonement of Jesus Christ can also be described by what it achieved—the possibility of our at-one-ment.

Because of Christ's Atonement and Resurrection, the at-one-ment of our bodies and spirits is assured (see 2 Nephi 9:10–12). Because of the Atonement of Jesus Christ, we can gain our integrity by receiving strength to do right things even when it is difficult to do so. Because of the Atonement of Jesus Christ, we can be brought to at-one-ment with others by having our hearts filled with His mercy. Because of the Atonement of Jesus Christ we can see the mark for which we are striving to achieve by having our minds enlightened with His Light and Truth. Because of the Atonement of Jesus Christ we have a perfect vision of the works we are to do, those that we saw and read about Him doing.

President Joseph Fielding Smith one time compared our journey through life and our mistakes to falling into a pit from which unaided we cannot escape. In the pit we are separated from the freedom to progress and denied opportunities to be one with others. The Atonement of Jesus Christ is in effect a ladder let down into the pit. If we accept the offered gift, we can use it to climb to freedom.[3] If we ignore the ladder, it fails to benefit our efforts to progress on our journey and to enjoy the society of those from whom we are separated by our confinement in the pit (see Alma 21:9; 34:9).

Every commandment, including the commandment to "be one," comes with promised blessings. So what are the promised blessings associated with the commandment to "be one"? The promised blessings include conversion, membership in Zion, and salvation and joy as we progress because of our own efforts and Christ's grace wrought through His infinite Atonement (see 2 Nephi 25:23).

President Joseph F. Smith reflected on this blessing of at-one-ment—our being saved because of the Atonement of Jesus Christ. "On the third of October, in the year nineteen hundred and eighteen, I sat in my room pondering over the scriptures; and reflecting upon the great atoning sacrifice that was made by the Son of God, for the redemption of the world; and the great and wonderful love made manifest by the Father and the Son in the coming of the Redeemer into the world; that through his atonement, and by obedience to the principles of the gospel, mankind might be saved" (D&C 138:1–4).

But from what are we saved by our own best efforts and through Christ's Atonement? The answer is, from sorrowful separations. For example, we are saved from the separation of our bodies and spirits when they are reunited in a condition of at-one-ment at the time of the resurrection. We are saved from the separation caused by sin when through repentance and Christ's Atonement we are worthy to come again into God's presence and be at-one with Him. We are saved from separations between siblings when we replace hard feelings with soft hearts that feel and stimulate service. We are saved from the conflict between the desires of the natural man and the Lord's spirit within us when we are strengthened by Christ's grace and put off the natural man and become converted. All of these saved conditions are made possible because of Christ's Atonement and our keeping the commandment to be one.

If we choose to disobey God and ignore His commandments, then we will suffer the alone-ment referred to in the scriptures as spiritual death, a vivid metaphor for the separations that accompany sin (see Helaman 14:17–18). In contrast, if we are like lambs who hearken to and approach the voice of the Good Shepherd, then He will draw near to us and enfold us in His love (see 1 Nephi 22:25). And even when we make mistakes and sin and enter into the wilderness like a lost lamb, He seeks to redeem and bring us back (see Luke 15:4–6).

The message of the restored gospel is to "come unto Christ" and be saved. Nephi, one of the twelve disciples of Christ living at the time of His coming to the Americas wrote that "the Lamb of God is the Son of the Eternal Father, and the Savior of the world; and that all men must come unto him, or they cannot be saved" (1 Nephi 13:40). The Savior admonishes, "Draw near unto me and I will draw near unto you; seek me diligently and ye shall find me; ask, and ye shall receive; knock, and it shall be opened unto you" (D&C 88:63).

We are commanded to love God and man, and to be one. These are connected commandments. We become one with God, man, and our best selves as we love one another as God has loved us. Our efforts to be one with God begin by our keeping His commandments, always remembering Him, and by returning to Him through repentance when we have rebelled against Him through sin. We strive to be one with others by leading them to the love of God by sharing with them His gospel. We also attend to their physical needs by sharing what we have with those who have not. If we do those things that promote at-one-ments between men and God, then we experience joy.

Elder Tad Callister explains that our connection to Christ's Atonement will require that we employ all of our senses.

> An attempt to master this doctrine [of atonement] requires an immersion of all our senses, all of our feelings, and all our intellect. Given the opportunity, the Atonement will invade each of the human passions and faculties, and in so doing will invite an exhaustion of each in order to more fully grasp its meaning. Those who have refined their cultural sensitivities will approach the Atonement with a more heart-felt empathy for the tenderness and compassion it represents. Those who have sacrificed their lives in service will stand in even greater awe of Him who sacrificed his all. Those who have perfected the powers of reason will probe with even deeper insight in the "whys" and "hows," not just the consequences of this intensely sublime doctrine.[4]

So now let us speak of the Atonement of Christ and strive to obtain a perfect knowledge of Christ and of our possibilities to be like Him and with Him in the world to come (see Jacob 4:12). To become like and one with the Savior we must follow His path and *become* at-one with Him in our minds (wisdom), in our capacity to do good deeds (stature), and in our at-one-ment (favor) with God and man that depends on our softened heart and enlightened vision (see Luke 2:52).

The gospel means literally the "good news." But what is the good news? That all mankind may be saved by obedience to the laws and ordinances included in the plan of happiness—and all this is possible because of the Atonement of Jesus Christ.

A Personal Note

As the year 2007 began, Bonnie and I were confidently looking forward to the last six months of our three-year assignment to preside over the Spain Malaga Mission. To be honest, we were convinced that we could finish with a flourish. And why not? At the beginning of our mission we had supervised the implementation of the Church's major new missionary program described in *Preach My Gospel*. We had learned to live through transfers, training meetings, and challenges to the health and well-being of our missionaries. We had experienced major changes in our missionary complements that left us at one point with nearly one-half of our missionaries training new missionaries.

We had learned how to extend our ministry and administration to include the members and missionaries in the Canary Islands—what had been before the Spain Las Palmas Mission. We had survived a major traffic accident that put Bonnie in the hospital and then suffered the devastation of having one of our finest missionaries die in the mission field. Finally, we had witnessed the miracle of seeing the Lord bless us with double the converts per missionary compared to our first year in the mission field. "Yes," we said to each other, "we have seen it all and we can surely finish with a flourish."

Then I had the impression to have a delayed medical examination that revealed a highly elevated PSA (Prostate Specific Antigen) score. After learning of my medical test results, the Church medical team directed us to return immediately to Salt Lake City for a biopsy that confirmed my having prostate cancer.

We were devastated, not only by our serious medical problem, but by the separation from our beloved missionaries and members. We were jolted from a life filled with daily missionary duties that enriched our lives to mostly waiting for the results of more medical tests. Yet, with the love of our members, missionaries, friends, and our children who all came to comfort us, we survived those early weeks.

Then life settled into a routine. We returned to Michigan and I resumed my academic work at Michigan State University. Yet part of my routine included reporting for daily radiation treatments at Ingham Regional Medical Oncology Center.

At first I felt alone at the hospital, but then I started to notice others facing the same treatments I faced. These new friends included Jim, who having lost all of his hair, smiled with divine patience; Les, senior to me, but whose gentle humor made fun of the whole event; Sarah, a young and cheerful mother who laughed so whole-heartedly that no one would ever know of her challenges; Sharman who through some genetic quirk found herself and four other members of her immediate family with cancer; and finally, Arnold, who flatly faced his cancer by declaring without bitterness, "You have to take the hand you're dealt."

I share this experience because of the insight it has provided me about the Savior. What I learned is that shared afflictions can create powerful bonds. I have been humbled by the bonds I have forged with my fellow oncology patients through our shared trials. I know what they are feeling and suffering, and I know they know what trials I am passing through—and in the midst of these shared trials comes a feeling of love. Yes, shared suffering and love seem to be powerful partners.[5]

I lean on this experience to help me appreciate the at-one-ment that exists between me and my Savior. He suffered with me and for me. He knows what I have felt like when I have stumbled and suffered. And because He knows my deepest distress, I know He loves me completely and, in my own limited way, I love Him in return and humbly offer my gratitude for His sacrifices that help me hope that I can become more like Him.

Conclusions

The poet John Donne wrote of our at-one-ment, "No man is an island entire of itself; every man is a piece of the continent, a part of the main. If a clod be washed away by the sea, Europe is the less, as well as if a promontory were, as well as if a manor of thy friend's or of thine own were. Any man's death diminishes me, because I am involved in mankind, and therefore never send to know for whom the bell tolls; it tolls for thee."[6]

Christ's Atonement brings at-one-ment to all that is virtuous, lovely, or of good report or praiseworthy.[7] Without the at-one-ment of questions, and answers provided by and through the Atonement of Jesus Christ, our lives lack meaning and joy. Without Christ's Atonement there are sins man cannot erase, mistakes he cannot forget, relationships he cannot mend, and hopes he cannot hold to. No wonder we call Christ's infinite sacrifice through which all things hold together the great "at-one-ment."

Finally, because of the Atonement of Jesus Christ we have a ship in which we can sail together in a sea of separations. Paul declared, "For I am persuaded, that neither death, nor life, nor angels, nor principalities, nor powers, nor things present, nor things to come, nor height, nor depth, nor any other creature, shall be able to separate us from the love of God, which is in Christ Jesus our Lord" (Romans 8:38–39).

Joseph Smith taught that every principle of the gospel, which includes the principle of at-one-ment, is an appendage to the Atonement of Jesus Christ.[8] This prophetic insight suggests an analogy—God's plan of happiness can be likened to a wheel with spokes and a rim. The Atonement of Jesus Christ may be likened to the hub of the wheel.[9] Gospel principles and ordinances are like the spokes of the wheel connected to this hub. Commandments and covenants of the gospel that put into effect gospel principles and ordinances are like the rim of the wheel that carries us to promised blessings. Just as the spokes of a wheel could not sustain the wheel's rim unless connected to its hub, so too would gospel principles and ordinances be unable to sustain our travel to the promised blessings of at-one-ment unless held together by the Atonement of Jesus Christ. The purpose of the gospel wheel—Christ's Atonement, gospel principles, ordinances, commandments, and covenants—are to carry us to the promised condition of at-one-ment.

And finally, to our Father in Heaven, we pray in song for our final at-one-ment, "At length when [we've] completed all you sent [us] forth to do, with your mutual approbation let [us] come and dwell with you."[10]

NOTES

1. Gordon B. Hinckley, "In These Three I Believe," *Ensign*, July 2006, 2–8.

2. Gordon B. Hinckley, "The Father, Son, and Holy Ghost," *Ensign*, March 1998, 2–7.

3. Joseph Fielding Smith, *Doctrines of Salvation*, comp. Bruce R. McConkie, 3 vols. (1954–56),1:126–127.

4. Tad R. Callister, Infinite *Atonement*, (2000), 1–2.

5. Since completing my treatments, my prostate cancer appears to be in remission and I am enjoying wonderful health. I hope for the same for my friends whom I have described.

6. John Donne, *Devotions upon Emergent Occasions*, XVII: Meditation, 1624.

7. The Pearl of Great Price, "The Articles of Faith of the Church of Jesus Christ of Latter-day Saints," 60–61.

8. *Teachings of the Prophet Joseph Smith*, sel. Joseph Fielding Smith, (1974), 121.

9. Robert L. Millet, *The Power of the Word: Saving Doctrines from the Book of Mormon*, (1994), 206.

10. "O My Father," *Hymns of The Church of Jesus Christ of Latter-day Saints*, no. 138.